# Battleground

# OPERATION PLUNDER
## Rhine Crossing

## THE BRITISH & CANADIAN OPERATIONS

"Me sir? looting sir?"

# Battleground series:

# Battleground Europe

# OPERATION PLUNDER
## Rhine Crossing

---

# THE BRITISH & CANADIAN OPERATIONS

Tim Saunders

Pen & Sword
**MILITARY**

First published in Great Britain in 2006 by
Pen & Sword Military
an imprint of
Pen & Sword Books Ltd
47 Church Street
Barnsley
South Yorkshire
S70 2AS

**ISBN 1 84415 221 9**

A CIP catalogue record for this book is
available from the British Library.

Typeset in Palatino

Printed and bound in the United Kingdom by CPI

Pen & Sword Books Ltd incorporates the imprints of Pen & Sword Aviation, Pen
& Sword Maritime, Pen & Sword Military, Wharncliffe Local History, Pen and
Sword Select, Pen and Sword Military Classics and Leo Cooper.
For a complete list of Pen & Sword titles, please contact
Pen & Sword Books Limited
47 Church Street, Barnsley, South Yorkshire, S70 2AS, England
E-mail: enquiries@pen-and-sword.co.uk
Website: www.pen-and-sword.co.uk

# CONTENTS

# Introduction

Operation PLUNDER was the overall name for 21st Army Group's crossing of the Rhine but each of the major elements was known by its own codeword, TURNSCREW and TORCHLIGHT, the British assault river crossings; WIGEON, the attack by 1 Commando Brigade on Wesel and FLASHLIGHT, the crossing by XVI US Corps. Operation VARSITY, the airborne drop east of the river, was also a component of PLUNDER but 6th British Airborne Division's part will be covered in a separate *Battleground* volume, as will the American crossings immediately south of Wesel. Consequently, this book concentrates on the part played by the British XII and XXX Corps during Operation PLUNDER.

The Rhine Crossing was the last great set piece battle of the North West European Campaign. It was an immensely complicated operation launched in less than a month and just two weeks after the First Canadian Army reached the Rhine at Wesel. Second British Army, who were to command the crossing, was now a veteran formation, very different in character from that which landed in Normandy during June and July 1944. The headquarter staffs and the largely citizen officers and soldiers in the units they commanded, knew their jobs and realised that to finish the task they had to defeat the Germans.

Despite their mauling in the Battle of the Rhineland, defeating a resolute enemy whose only choice was unconditional surrender was never going to be easy. In addition, the Germans were defending their last strategic barrier, the mighty Rhine, which is three hundred yards wide between Rees and Wesel. The far bank was held by a mixture of troops, in the north, XXX Corps faced the fanatical *II Fallschirmjäger Korps*, while further south, XII Corps were opposed by the remains of *84th Volksgrenadier Division* and the old men and boys of Germany's last reserves. However, both German formations were supported by their own armour, as well as the reserve of panzers and panzer grenadiers from *XLVII Panzer Korps*, who could not be underestimated.

Operation PLUNDER is not without its controversies. Some critics of Montgomery's battle have criticised the resources consumed and the casualties incurred, particularly amongst the airborne forces but this operation was General Eisenhower's main effort. He had to get across the Rhine and deny the sustaining industrial capacity of the Ruhr to the enemy. 'Sneak attacks' across the river further to the south, could not deliver the knockout blow to Germany's industry and nor it seemed, could the Allied bomber forces.

As usual, there are points of language that need explaining. Firstly, the terms referring to the earthen banks built to contain the Rhine floods, used in equal measure by contemporary authors, are 'dyke' and 'bund'. The latter is one of many words taken into the British military lexicon as a result of service in India. Another interchangeable term is used to describe the amphibious landing craft used to take the infantry across the Rhine; the Landing Vehicle Tracked or LVT, which was also known in British service as the 'Buffalo'. Finally, the term D Day is not confined to the landings in Normandy on 6 June 1944 but is used to indicate the day on which a specific operation is to take place. In the case of Operation PLUNDER, D Day was 24 March 1945, with preliminary operations taking place on the evening of D-1, the 23rd.

# Acknowledgements

I would like to thank the Land Warfare Centre Library for access to their unrivalled collection of increasingly rare infantry regimental histories. These are absolutely essential in writing about an operation such as this. Kate – many thanks and a happy retirement.

Thanks and acknowledgements are due to Richard Hone, formerly of the REME who helped me with armoured vehicle aspects of this book. I am most grateful for his expert assistance, in an area that is not my forte.

I would also like to thank those authors, publishers, regiments and corps who have allowed me to quote freely from their works. Without their generous support, a book like this would not be possible. Fellow *Battleground* author Andrew Rawson helped me with copies of maps from the US National Archive. His timely assistance with these helped me greatly.

Finally, thanks are due to the headquarters and museums of the British Army regiments who forced the crossing of the Rhine, for their help in putting me in touch with veterans and making available documents and maps that have not been previously published. As ever it is a pleasure to speak to Canadian military headquarters and museums, who see it as their job to actively promote and disseminate their regiments' history. They give their time and resources freely, so many thanks are due to them and all those others who have helped make this book possible.

Whether at home or on the ground, enjoy the tour.

Tim Saunders
Warminster 2006

# CHAPTER ONE

# Background

IN EARLY SEPTEMBER 1944, following their victory in Normandy and pursuit across northern France, the Allies believed that final victory over Nazi Germany was close at hand. The Red Army, to the east, was inexorably closing on Germany; while the Allied air forces harried the *Wehrmacht* and did their best to obliterate the German industrial base and lines of communication. In the west, Allied armies were ranged from Switzerland to the North Sea, preparing for the final assault on Hitler's Germany.

Optimism ran high, with normally stoic intelligence officers predicting that victory against Germany was 'within sight, almost within reach' and they reported that it was 'unlikely that organised German resistance would continue beyond 1 December 1944'. Dissenting voices who believed that the German forces were not finished and were preparing a 'last-ditch struggle in the field at all costs', were, in the prevailing enthusiasm, ignored.

Montgomery's attempt, in Operation MARKET GARDEN, to 'bounce 21st Army Group across the Rhine onto the North German Plain' had demonstrated that the Germans were far from finished. There was to be no repeat of the 1918 German civil and military collapse after Normandy that many commanders who had served in the Great War predicted and no dash into the heart of Germany in 1944. Quite the reverse, for while the Allies clinched victory in Normandy and the British and American Armies streamed east across France, 200,000 mostly slave labourers, worked to strengthen the pre-war German defences known as the West Wall or Siegfried Line. The physical barrier was to be manned by new citizen or *volksgrenadier* formations, with Himmler calling to arms the young, the old and many men previously excluded from the *Wehrmacht* on grounds of economic necessity, health, etc. To these men were added the now largely redundant manpower from the *Luftwaffe* and *Kriegsmarine*. Together they were drafted into the new *volksgrenadier* divisions for the final defence of the

**Field Marshall Montgomery. Victor of Normandy but defeated at Arnhem.**

Third Reich. The Allies had and were to continue to underestimate the German genius for highly effective military improvisation and were largely unaware of the remarkable strategic recovery they were staging.

With the failure at Arnhem (Montgomery referred to it as a ninety percent success) General Eisenhower reverted to his broad front strategy. This favoured US doctrine (at the time) was also a politically acceptable policy that would see all three allied army groups closing up to the German frontier, breaching the Siegfried Line and then fighting their way to the Rhine, which was Germany's last strategic barrier. Destruction of the German field armies and the capture of the Ruhr, Germany's industrial

**General Eisenhower. Exercised a highly political command.**

powerhouse, were to be the principal targets rather than a headlong advance across the North German Plain to Berlin. The full impact of this policy rather than a dash east to Berlin was fully apparent to the British, who had an eye on the post-war situation in Europe, rather than simply an ending of the war against Germany in early 1945. In the increasingly bad autumn weather that heralded one of the worst winters for many years, the fighting was costly and Allied progress slowed to almost a halt. Nowhere was progress slower and more expensive in both British and American lives than at the Dutch town of Overloon in the Mass Pocket. Further to the north, the British fought to open the Scheldt Estuary and access to the vital port of Antwerp, which had to be open as the entry point for supplies in time for the final drive into Hitler's Reich. Elsewhere, desperate battles were fought by British and American troops to reach and then penetrate the Siegfried Line, at points such as Geilenkeirchen, where the British 43rd Wessex Division fought alongside the US 84th Division to overcome a determined enemy in weather and ground conditions that foreshadowed those they were to experience later in the winter of 44/45. Meanwhile, General Patton grumbled as his armour bogged down in the mud of Lorraine. The Germans fought with courage and determination to defend the borders of their Fatherland and it was clear that despite the continuing bomber offensive that the war was going to go on well into 1945.

**'Old Blood and Guts' General Patton.**

Hitler's counter-attack with his rebuilt army in the Ardennes in mid December 1944, launched under the cover of bad weather, caught the Allies by surprise. The German aim was to separate the Allied armies by striking north west to Antwerp, enveloping and destroying the US Ninth Army, along with the British and Canadian Armies. Initially, the Germans, benefiting from a lax American stance on a lightly held, quiet front, were successful and created a significant 'Bulge' in the Allied lines. However, the relatively inexperienced staffs of the Allied Armies of D Day were now honed to a high state of competence and reacted quickly to close off the German advance before they reached the River Meuse. With an improvement in the weather that allowed Allied airpower free reign, by the middle of January, the Germans were pushed back behind their lines of departure, with their reserves of men and material further depleted by their offensive. Meanwhile, the Russians had begun their attack on the Eastern Front and attempts to stem their advance were increasingly sucking German resources away from the west.

### The Winter War

Eisenhower, now fully aware of the German capacity for resistance, prepared operations, delayed by the Ardennes counter offensive, to dominate the Rhineland and to close up to the Rhine. SHAFE planners aimed to mount operations that were designed to destroy the main German field forces in the west before their remnants could withdraw across the river.

The fighting in early 1945 to reach the Rhine on a front from the Swiss border all the way north to Nijmegen is a subject in itself. In the north, Montgomery's 21st Army Group was to fight a massive and carefully planned battle (Operation VERITABLE)

**British infantry in the Ardennes but the snow had melted by the time of VERITABLE in the Rhineland.**

using General Crerar's First Canadian Army and General Simpson's Ninth US Army (Operation GRENADE). These operations were designed to reach the Rhine north of the Ruhr, while further south, First US Army delayed operations to capture the seven Roer dams. With the dams finally captured, First US Army's operations focused on crossing the River Ruhr and the reaching the Rhine around Cologne. Yet further south, Patton's Third US Army was to clear the difficult terrain east of the Ardennes, cross the River Moselle, fight through the Eiffel and reach the central sector of the Rhine between Coblenz and Mannheim. The southernmost Allied armies of 6th US Army Group, consisting of American and French divisions, who had already reached the Rhine near Strasbourg, were to breach the Siegfried Line and clear up significant pockets held by German divisions west of the Rhine.

While General Crerar's First Canadian Army was fighting the main body of the Germans in the west in the Battle of the Rhineland, the US army groups further to the south were approaching the Rhine across greater distances and some equally difficult terrain. First US Army reached the Rhine near

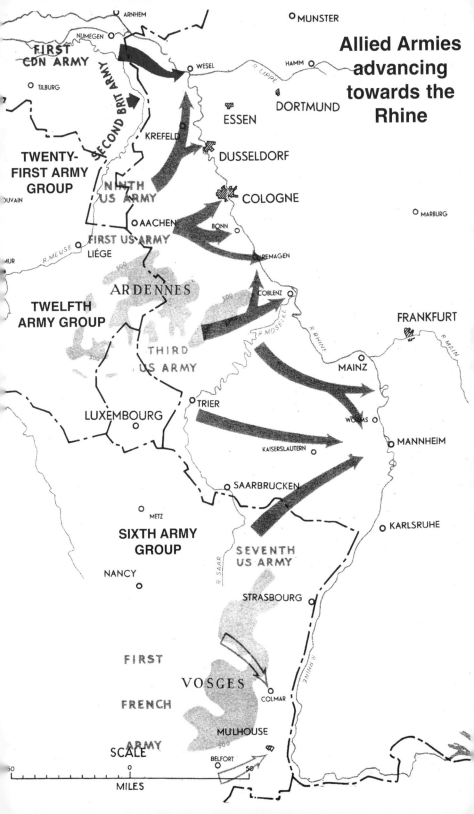

Cologne and days later, after numerous attempts to take a Rhine bridge by *coup de main*, on 7 March, the spearhead of 9th US Armoured Division, led by Lieutenant Karl Timmermans reached the Rhine further south and found the Ludendorf railway bridge at Remagen still standing. With the demolition guard lacking orders to blow the bridge, First US Army gained the honour of establishing the first Allied bridgehead across the Rhine. However, the country beyond the Remagen Bridgehead was so unsuitable for offensive operations and lacking strategically important objectives beyond, this was in reality a cul-de-sac of little strategic importance despite General Hodges (First US Army) pouring troops across. Perhaps the main effect of the Bridge's capture was to draw precious German divisions away from Eisenhower's main effort in the north.

The next crossing was further south and was of greater importance. General Omar Bradley, commander Twelfth US Army Group, recalls receiving a telephone call on the morning of 23 March at his HQ in Namur from General Patton's Third US Army HQ. His account illustrates the competition and vanity (both British and American) that now bedevilled Eisenhower's command.

*"Brad, don't tell anyone but I'm across."* I replied *"Well I'll*

**The Ludendorf Bridge at Remagen.**

be damned – you mean the Rhine?" "Sure do," he [Patton] *replied, "I sneaked a division over last night. But there are so few Krauts around they don't know it yet. So don't make any announcement – we'll keep it a secret until we see how it goes".*

Patton's formal situation report about his crossing at Nierstein pointedly included the statement that this had been achieved '... without the benefit of aerial bombing, ground smoke, artillery preparation, and airborne assistance, the Third Army at 2200 hours, Thursday evening March 22, crossed the River Rhine.' However, as Bradley recalled, 'That evening Patton telephoned again.'

*"Brad," he shouted and his treble voice trembled, "for God's sake tell the world we are across. We knocked down thirty-three Krauts* [aircraft] *today when they came after our*

**General Omar Bradley.**

*pontoon bridges. I want the world to know Third Army made it before Monty starts across".*

### Rhineland Operations of 21st Army Group

Meanwhile, with the limited British involvement on the northern flank of the Battle of the Bulge at an end, Montgomery turned his attention to the Rhineland in Operations VERITABLE, BLOCKBUSTER and GRENADE. He described the aims of the fighting west of the Rhine to close up to the great waterway between Xanten and Nijmegen.

*The object of the battle of the Rhineland was to destroy all enemy forces between the Rhine and the Meuse from the Nijmegen bridgehead as far south as the general line Julich-Düsseldorf, and subsequently to line up along the west bank of the Rhine with the Ninth US Army from Düsseldorf to Moers, Second* [British] *Army from Moers to Rees and* [First] *Canadian Army from exclusive Rees to Nijmegen.*

**21st Army Group's shoulder flash.**

This was to be achieved by First Canadian Army, with British formations under command, launching Operation VERITABLE; an attack south east from the Groesbeek Heights near Nijmegen,

15

which had been seized during MARKET GARDEN in September 1944. The Canadians' immediate objectives were the breaching of the Siegfried Line defences and clearance of the Reichswald forest. Subsequently they were to take the defended towns of Udem and Goch before heading south east to Geldern and Xanten where they would link up with Ninth US Army, who, in Operation GRENADE, would be advancing in a north easterly direction.

Facing 21st Army Group was General Schlemm, commander of the First *Fallschirmjäger* Army. He was experienced in holding operations, having been schooled in the art in the resource starved Italian theatre. Here he learnt to utilise terrain to maximise his defensive effect. However, on the Rhine Schlemm recounted that his orders were to hold the ground come what may:

> *Once the battle was joined, it was obvious that I no longer had a free hand in the conduct of the defence. My orders were that under no circumstances was any land between the Maas and the Rhine to be given up without permission of the Commander in Chief West, von Rundstedt, who in turn had to ask Hitler. For every withdrawal that I was forced to make due to an Allied attack, I had to send back a detailed explanation.*

Even so, Schlemm and other German commanders repeatedly requested that they be allowed to fall back to the Rhine where they could adopt strongly held positions. Instead, Hitler kept eighty-five divisions fighting west of the Rhine, forbidding any withdrawal and threatening to execute commanders who lost a bridge intact.

Starting on 8 February 1945, Operation VERITABLE and its continuation Operation BLOCKBUSTER are characterised by Brigadier Essame of 214 Brigade as:

> *... lasting for twenty-eight days and nights in almost unspeakable conditions of flood, mud and misery. The troops were soaked with almost incessant rain; there was no escaping it and no shelter. We met the First Parachute Army the last remaining German indoctrinated youth fighting with undiminished courage on German soil supported by 700 mortars and almost a thousand guns, on virtually equal terms.*

Fighting through the northern extensions of the Siegfried Line, which the Germans had five months to work on since the failure of MARKET GARDEN, was a costly business. The densely

Amphibious vehicles were at a premium in the flooded country between the Reichswald and the Rhine.

wooded and heavily fortified Reichswald, the defended towns, such as Udem and Goch, and the positions in depth (the Hochwald layback) took a month to fight through. The level of destruction of the German homeland, as he entered the ruins of Cleve, was recorded by a seasoned member of 4th Wiltshires:

*There were craters and fallen trees everywhere, bomb craters*

A British infantry company HQ and specialist armour in the Reichswald during Operation VERITABLE.

*packed so tight that the debris from one was piled against the rim of the next in a pathetic heap of rubble, roofs and radiators. There was not an undamaged house anywhere, piles of smashed furniture, clothing, children's books and toys, everything, was spilled in hopeless confusion amidst the bombed skeletons of the town.*

Infantry from Canada, the West Country, Wales and Scotland bore the brunt of the costly fighting through the ruined towns and the sodden country.

General Simpson's Ninth US Army was formally under operational command of 21st Army Group for the clearance of the Rhineland in operation GRENADE but the degree of influence Montgomery was able to exert by this stage over US forces under his command was strictly limited. Simpson's objective was the seizure of the Rhine's western bank, from where his army would in subsequent operations strike at the northern edge of the Ruhr. However, delays in starting his attack resulted from floodwaters in the river valley and First US

**Ninth Army's badge.**

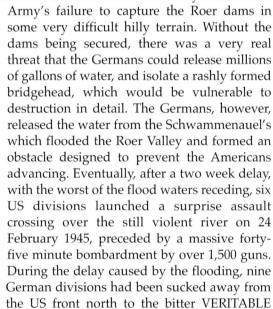

Army's failure to capture the Roer dams in some very difficult hilly terrain. Without the dams being secured, there was a very real threat that the Germans could release millions of gallons of water, and isolate a rashly formed bridgehead, which would be vulnerable to destruction in detail. The Germans, however, released the water from the Schwammenauel's which flooded the Roer Valley and formed an obstacle designed to prevent the Americans advancing. Eventually, after a two week delay, with the worst of the flood waters receding, six US divisions launched a surprise assault crossing over the still violent river on 24 February 1945, preceded by a massive forty-five minute bombardment by over 1,500 guns. During the delay caused by the flooding, nine German divisions had been sucked away from the US front north to the bitter VERITABLE

**General Simpson.**

battle being fought by General Crerar's troops. This contributed to the US assault divisions losing fewer than a hundred men

18

**US combat engineers struggle to maintain a footbridge across the swollen River Roer.**

killed in action on the first day of the assault.

With VERITABLE, GRENADE and the advance of the First US Army under way, a programme of air operations on a large scale was being conducted by the Allied tactical and bomber commands. 'This was designed to weaken the German defence as a whole, and to assist Twenty-First Army Group and Twelfth Army Group in particular, by the isolation and reduction of the Ruhr's war-making capacity.' According to the British Official History, the principal aims were, firstly:

> ... to isolate the Ruhr from central and southern Germany by cutting the main railways ..., secondly, to attack continuously west of that line the enemy's communications and transport system; and, thirdly, to prepare the battle area for the impending Rhine crossing by Twenty-First Army Group.

The official historian concluded that: 'In the next few weeks much of the industrial power of the Ruhr was dissipated in the dust of explosions from a rain of bombs which fell almost daily from the air.'

**One of Germany's airfields receives a pounding.**

Meanwhile, Simpson drove his men on to the Rhine and with massive US material strength his divisions poured over nineteen pontoon bridges over the Roer and:

> The enemy's resistance was soon characteristic of a general retreat in which only an attempt could be made to delay the Allied advance by holding road junctions and communications centres in key towns or villages, using in each case a number of assault and anti-aircraft guns and mortars and groups of supporting infantry.

As planned, the 35th US Division met up with Montgomery's 53rd Welsh Division at Geldern, mid-afternoon on 3 March and together the armies advanced east, squeezing a force of nominally fifteen German divisions belonging to First *Fallschirmjäger* Army, into a rapidly reducing bridgehead. Hitler would not sanction their withdrawal despite General Schlemm's protestations, who, in his post war interrogation, commented that once he was hemmed in to a shrinking bridgehead whose perimeter ran from Xanten, the Bonninghardtwald to the Rhine at Moers: 'I could see my hopes for a long life rapidly dwindling, since I had nine bridges in my sector!' A verbatim note in the Fuhrer Conference records gives Hitler's reasoning in response to a suggestion that they

**German infantry fighting alongside a Tiger tank in the Rhineland.**

redeploy east of the Rhine. 'I want him to hang on to the West Wall as long as is humanly possible, since withdrawal would merely mean moving the catastrophe from one place to another.'

Eventually, with Hitler's threat of execution hanging over him, Schlemm authorised, on his own initiative, the withdrawal of what manpower he could save before blowing the Wesel bridges. Montgomery's armies reached the Rhine in the area chosen for the crossing of the Rhine, Operation PLUNDER, on 5 March 1945, having suffered a total of 23,000 casualties in First Canadian and Ninth US Armies.

The Battle of the Rhineland, however, had cost General Schlemm's First *Fallschirmjäger* Army between 90,000 and 100,000 men, with casualties being largely concentrated amongst nineteen infantry divisions, which were now reduced to little more than cadres. The fighting west of the Rhine cost von Rundstedt, C-in-C West, half a million men and for the third time, his job. At the age of seventy, he could finally retire knowing that he had delayed the enemy more successfully than any commander and that the end would be not long in coming.

*Feldmarschall* **von Rundstedt, sacked for the final time.**

## The Strategic Situation

It is widely accepted that Hitler's decision to remain fighting west of the Rhine, Germany's last strategic barrier, was a major mistake that probably shortened the war by a few weeks, compounding as it did, earlier errors. By gathering the majority of his best troops for the Ardennes offensive, Hitler had also left Germany open to the Soviet Winter offensive launched by Zhukov and Koniev. In the east, facing a five to one superiority in men and material, the German front collapsed and the Red Army, driven on by Stalin's threats and blandishments, advanced some 250 miles to a point as close as forty miles from Berlin, where running out of steam they were eventually halted by last ditch German resistance. Meanwhile, at the Yalta Conference, the Allies were

**One of the last photographs taken of Hitler as he distributes the Iron Cross to members of the Hitler Youth defending Berlin.**

only able to report to Stalin that they had restored their lines of the previous November.

The Ardennes offensive had cost Hitler his last strategic and operational reserves, which arguably could have lengthened the war by several months. With, in addition, the losses suffered during the Rhineland Battles, the *Wehrmacht* was in March 1945 only capable of standing on the defensive. As Eisenhower wrote, with the benefit of hindsight '... the enemy was now in no condition to hold fast in the defended line to which he had been compelled to retreat'. The end indeed would not be long in coming but the Rhine and the heavily defended Ruhr would first have to be overcome to knock Germany out of the war.

### Second British Army

At the end of Operation VERITABLE, after nine months of active campaigning, the British Army that had crossed the German border and was about to take part in the last major

Allied offensive of the war, was very different from the army that had landed in Normandy. Brigadier Essame of 43rd Wessex Division wrote of the state of the British 2nd Army at the end of March 1945:

*Despite exposure twenty-four hours a day for over a month, to the almost incessant rain and sleet and intense and sustained enemy fire, the morale of the British troops as the battle progressed rose, rather than declined, to a higher level than at any stage during the campaign.*

**Second British Army.**

This seemingly counter intuitive statement is supported by the fact that the number of Second Army soldiers reporting sick was at an all time low in February and March 1944 and the incidence of psychiatric casualties had declined markedly. Essame accounts for this phenomenon as '... men, the majority of whom had been new to the horrors of the battlefield in Normandy, had now got into their stride and had become inured to the sights and smells of the battlefield.'

Not only were Montgomery's troops in better mental and physical shape but they had become experienced campaigners. An officer of the Dorset Regiment who had been wounded in Normandy returned to his battalion in time for the Rhine crossing and found his company greatly changed from the formally dressed and inexperienced unit he left in August 1944.

*It was a tonic to find oneself again in the free air of good comradeship, cooperation and good humoured stoicism of the front line after months of jealousies and petty rivalries so rampant further back ... The company looked a truly amazing sight as we marched into our concentration area. The men were loaded down with the usual impedimenta of ammunition, weapons, picks and shovels; but then in addition, every man had some personal treasure; some had hurricane lamps, some oil house lamps or an oil stove, others carried baskets and two*

**General Sir Miles Dempsey, commander Second Army.**

*whole sections arrived each with some joint of the pig they had killed the day before slung across their haversacks. They looked a motley crew in a variety of battledress, leather jerkins or camouflage jackets, topped with weather beaten faces and a range of scarves but they knew their trade as soldiers and they could be relied on in battle; that was all that mattered.*

The practicalities of everyday life on campaign were not the only changes in the British Army. The green formations, such as 15th Scottish and 43rd Wessex Divisions, who had seen their first action in Normandy, were now made up of experienced combat soldiers and were highly competent; from divisional staff down to the rifle sections, they knew their tasks in battle and understood that the only way to return to their families was to finish the war. Similarly, the desert veterans of 51st Highland Division, who had been criticised for their poor performance in Normandy and, for a while, labelled as one of the 'non fighting divisions', had been restored to their former level of performance and determination to win, largely by its new commander Major General Thomas Rennie.

The worst of the infantry manpower crisis of the autumn had also passed. Men were ruthlessly combed out of units in the UK that were now largely redundant. The organisations that bore the brunt of this process were typically, those who earlier in the war provided Britain with her air defence. Anti-aircraft gunners found themselves converted to infantry and undergoing a crash course in small arms and close quarter battle. RAF radar operator, Corporal Southam found himself one of the thousands drawing khaki battledress and joining the Army.

*I was surprised that I took to the army, especially as it was mid-winter when I reported to Barnard Castle for infantry training. The discomfort of living in the field more than made up for escaping from the boredom of routine RAF shift work on an air station in the middle of nowhere.*

Southam was lucky, he was posted direct to a battalion but others, usually less enthusiastic about their transformation to the dangers and discomforts of life as an infantryman, suffered the misfortune of having to wait in the uninspiring environment of a battle casualty replacement unit.

Also joining the order of battle for the coming Rhine Crossing was 6th Airborne Division. They had since their withdrawal from Normandy at the end of the battle, plenty of time to retrain and take in replacements to make good the losses of a hundred days in close contact, with the enemy. Their austere Christmas 1944 celebrations in their camps on Salisbury Plain were cancelled by an emergency deployment to the Ardennes as a part of the force to block the German drive on the Meuse and their ultimate objective; Antwerp. The veteran airborne division, now under a new British airborne commander, Major General Eric Bols were ready for the battle again. Their former commander, the experienced Lieutenant General 'Windy' Gale, however, would not be far away, as he was deputy commander of the Allied Airborne Army.

In summary, costly though the Rhineland battles had been, the British, American and Canadian armies were well led and their soldiers had endured the worst of the winter. With battle casualty replacements swelling their ranks, they knew that victory was inevitable, despite the motivational cautioning of their officers. With logistic superiority and air supremacy to support them, the only real question was when it all would end. Conversely, as we will see in the next chapter, the Germans after the Battle of the Bulge and the losses suffered facing VERITABLE and GRENADE, were in a parlous state.

**Victory for the Allies was certain, the remaining question was 'when'. British infantry pass a column of German prisoners.**

# CHAPTER 2

# The German Defenders

DEFEATED IN NORMANDY, the Germans belatedly took measures to put their economy and nation onto a total war footing. Places of entertainment were closed, non-essential activities curtailed and men and women were directed into crucial industries and into the *Wehrmacht*. Within the forces, as already mentioned, men were taken from the now largely redundant *Kriegsmarine* and from the bloated ranks of Goering's *Luftwaffe*. The results were spectacular. Germany's armoured vehicle production reached a peak despite the best efforts of the Allied bomber offensive and divisions such as the 84th Infantry, who Second Army were to face on the banks of the Rhine, were reconstituted following its virtual destruction at Falaise. Others became *volksgrenadier* divisions made up of Germany's last reserves. The best of the reconstituted formations were sent to the Siegfried Line along with two thirds of all armoured production.

**Young and old, along with party officials, were swept up into the ranks of the new German Army in a last ditch defence of the Fatherland.**

Despite rebuilding the *Wehrmacht* in a matter of months, this was not the same quality of Army as before, being made up of a high proportion of men who would previously have been regarded as too old, too young or had a physical infirmity that would previously have excluded them from service. The better 'divisions', in many cases, consisted of two regiments (equivalent to a British brigade) each of two infantry battalions with little transport. Artillery was short but this deficiency was made up by a generous allocation of mortars and multi-barrel rocket launchers; the *Nebelwerfer*, which was a major cause of allied casualties. German small arms firepower, was however, largely undiminished with an equally generous allocation of MG 34 and MG 42 *spandau*s in infantry battalions.

### Volkssturm

At the lower end of the scale, the weakest formations were based on the *Volkssturm*; the old and sick men of the German Home Guard, with in some cases their only uniform being an arm-band. The commanding officer of 41st *Volkssturm* Battalion described what occurred when his unit was sent into battle early in March. Although an extreme case, his story is generally representative of what happened to many battalions such as his.

*I had 400 men in my battalion and we were ordered to go into the line in our civilian clothes. I told the local Party Leader that I could not accept the*

**Goebbels inspects a mixed *Volkssturm* unit of the type that was rejected after the Ardennes offensive.**

*responsibility of leading men into battle without uniforms or much training. Just before commitment the unit was given 180 Danish rifles, but there was no ammunition. We also had four machine guns and 100* Panzerfausts. *None of the men had received any training in firing a machine gun, and they were all afraid of handling the anti-tank weapon. Although my men were quite ready to help their country, they refused to go into battle without uniforms and without training. What can a* Volkssturm *man do with a rifle without ammunition! The men went home. That was the only thing they could do.*

## The Hitler Youth

The younger soldiers recruited from the Hitler Youth (HJ), despite their lack of age, were often good and dedicated material. However, in the Ardennes the *Volksgrenadier* division's HJ soldiers had not performed to their potential, as the Normandy Veterans and older *Volkssturm* knew it was 'all up for Germany' and encouraged the boys – for that is what they were – to surrender. Consequently, the HJ leadership decided to keep HJ conscripts, some of whom were boys as young as twelve years of age, in separate units, rarely more than a hundred strong.

By keeping the boys in their own HJ units, with fanatical Nazi leadership, they were able to exploit the qualities brought about by years of indoctrination, along with those of youth that makes warfare a young man's game. Many went willingly, with patriotism and the gullibility of youth; believing Goebbels' propaganda that Hitler's 'wonder weapons' and one last push would turn the tide and ultimately deliver victory to the Fatherland. Of all the Nazi deceptions perpetrated on the German people this was possibly the most cynical and evil of them all.

Even though they had little formal recruit training, most of the HJ had received, along with Nazi indoctrination, years of military training during routine HJ meetings and camps. This 'training', with weapons and ammunition, often re-enacting German victories earlier in the war, laid a solid military foundation but in reality, as with the *Volkssturm* they lacked weapons and equipment. However, the spirit was willing and HJ units from the Rhineland were prepared to defend their hometowns with what ever they had. The *Panzerfausts* proved to

29

*Hitler Jugend* recruits in late 1944 were facing the enemy in a matter of weeks.

**Some well equipped *Hitler Jugend* soldiers. In most cases this was far from the reality by late March 1945.**

be an effective weapon even in the hands of novices.

HJ units were amongst those rushed to the banks of the Rhine from the nearby Ruhr and were encountered, along with other troop types, across the PLUNDER battle area but particularly in Wesel.

### *Fallschirmjäger*

The SS *panzer* divisions, now deployed to the east to stem the Russian offensive, and the *Fallschirmjäger* alone retained much of their former quality. The latter provided the backbone of the German defences in the Rhineland and were the major opponents of the British and Canadian forces during VERITABLE and BLOCKBUSTER. Mostly aged under twenty-five these troops were parachutists in name only, mostly having never been trained to jump but, nurtured on the deeds of their forebears at Crete, Cassino, etc. they had an *esprit de corps* that the *Wehrmacht* had long since lost. Also, with many men coming from *Luftwaffe* stations, they had not tasted the bitter pill of defeat and their tenacity in the fighting in early 1945 may have had a lot to do with the fact that only unconditional surrender by Germany was on the table and they had little choice but to continue resisting.

Veteran *Fallschirmjäger,* and persistent thorn in the Allied side, *Oberstleutnant* von der Hydte left the text of his early 1945 speech to new recruits joining his regiment:

*Oberstleutnant* **von der Hydte, a persistent thorn in the Allies' side from 1940 through Crete and Normandy to Hell's Highway.**

*I demand of every soldier the renunciation of all personal wishes. Whoever swears on the Prussian flag has no right to personal possessions! From the moment he enlists in the* Fallschirmjäger *and comes to my regiment, every soldier enters the new order of humanity and gives up everything he possessed before and which is outside the new order. There is only one law henceforth for him – the law of our unit. He must abjure every weaker facet of his own character, all personal ambition, and every personal desire. From the renunciation of the individual, the true personality of the soldier arises. Every member of the regiment must know what he is fighting for.*

*He must be quite convinced that this struggle is a struggle for the existence of the whole German nation and that no other ending of this battle is possible than that of the victory of German arms... . He must learn to believe in victory even when at certain moments logical thinking scarcely makes a German victory seem possible... . Only the soldier who is schooled in philosophy and believes in his political faith implicitly can fight as this war demands that he shall fight. ... lack of this faith is the reason why so many German infantry divisions have been destroyed.*

In summary, despite the presence of the committed *Fallschirmjäger,* overall the *Wehrmacht,* as demonstrated by the Battle of the Bulge was no longer capable of successfully mounting major offensive operations. There were too few first class formations, panzer divisions were armoured largely in name only and of course, the Allies were no longer the bemused

32

force of 1940 that was so easily overwhelmed by Hitler's blitzkrieg.

**Defence on the Rhine**

Charged with holding the Rhine, as Hitler's new C-in-C West, was the stocky, blunt jawed and resolute *Generalfeldmarschall* Albert Kesselring. He had gained a reputation as a defensive genius fighting delaying actions in Italy on the Gustav and Gothic Lines. Arriving in his new headquarters he reputedly announced to his staff 'Well gentlemen, I am the new V3'. On the Rhine the policy 'Laughing Albert' had to implement remained focussed on the defence of the Ruhr, which following the loss of Upper Silesia to the Russians was the last industrial area, vital to sustain German forces in action. To achieve this, Kesselring had nominally sixty-five divisions but in reality they had a strength of less than half this number.

*Feldmarschall* **Kesselring, known as 'Laughing Albert', the self confessed 'V3 weapon'.**

Despite an acute weapons shortage and the crippling blows German industry and communications were receiving from the Allied air forces, Kesselring managed to put together a creditable defence to oppose the expected assault crossing of the Rhine. However, this defence was less strong than Montgomery believed he would encounter, based on the experience of the bitter fighting during VERITABLE and BLOCKBUSTER.

General Schlemm's First *Fallschirmjäger* Army remained responsible for the sector opposite 21st Army Group, including the Rees–Wesel sector. During his post war interrogation Schlemm explained that:

> *A parachute drop over the Rhine was considered inevitable, and efforts were made to determine the most probable spot. Schlemm had captured an Allied report analysing the parachute drop at Arnhem in September 1944, and from this document, he*

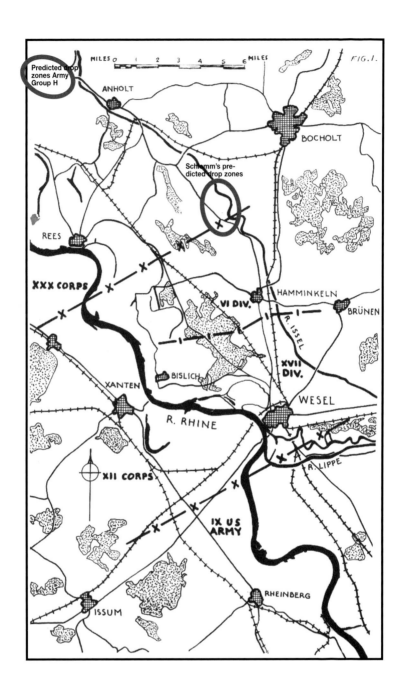

FIG. 1.

Predicted drop zones Army Group H

Schlemm's predicted drop zones

MILES 0 1 2 3 4 5 6 MILES

ANHOLT

BOCHOLT

REES

XXX CORPS

HAMMINKELN

VI DIV.

BRÜNEN

R. ISSEL

XVII DIV.

BISLICH

XANTEN

WESEL

R. RHINE

XII CORPS

R. LIPPE

IX US ARMY

RHEINBERG

ISSUM

*learnt that Allied views were now against a paratroop landing too far away from the ground troops destined to contact it. By plotting the areas that were topographically suitable for a parachute drop and not too far from the Rhine, Schlemm claims the most likely area seemed to be just east of Wesel. It was in this neighbourhood that he therefore expected the crossing attempt would be made.*

**General Schlemm.**

Schlemm's views however were not considered sound by his superiors at Army Group H:

*The expected northern crossing was to take place, according to these latter opinions, in the neighbourhood of Emmerich. The assault would be directed north-east and designed to take the Ijssel line in the rear. Since this was to be the big attack, Schlemm was ordered to send a large part of his artillery to Twenty-Fifth Army who would be faced with this new offensive.*

As subsequent events would prove, this was a miscalculation of some significance and Schlemm's deployment on the Rhine with two corps and an armoured reserve was, as was the case with the Germans pre-D Day dispositions, a compromise. *II Fallschirmjäger Korps* were deployed in the north, with *6, 7* and *8 Fallschirmjäger Divisions* astride the town of Rees. In what was to become the right assault sector of Second British Army, Schlemm had deployed General Straube's *LXXXVI Korps* centred on Wesel, with 84th and 180th Divisions under command. Schlemm's armoured reserve, *XLVII Panzer Korps*, was located fifteen miles to the north east of Emmerich. *116th Panzer Division* was assessed by allied intelligence on 22 March, as having up to seventy tanks, while *15th Panzer Grenadiers* was believed to hold fifteen panzers and twenty to thirty assault guns.

The divisions directly facing the British assault were *8th Fallschirmjäger* and *84th Infantry Division*. *7th Fallschirmjäger Division* had not been properly located but some of its units were known to be well forward. The former was on the left of *II Fallschirmjäger Korps* and had lost heavily in the fighting west of

**The best of the men and equipment were concentrated in armoured formations, including anti-airlanding battlegroups. In this case they are mounted in an armoured half-track.**

the Rhine and when it withdrew across the line in early March, it had an infantry strength of just 900 men. *84th Division*, a luckless formation under the command of *Generalmajor* Fiebig, had been virtually destroyed, for the second time, at the beginning of VERITABLE and was assessed on 12 March, as having a strength of just 500 infantrymen. However, it was in the process of being reconstituted as a mountain formation when PLUNDER started on the night of 23/24 March. Amongst those who had already arrived to join the beleaguered division were some *Volkssturm* (German Home Guard), some static *Wehrkreis* (German military district) troops (possibly *317 Ersatz Battalion* in Wesel and those troops encountered around Bislich) and amongst others, *286th Ear Battalion*, made up of soldiers who were deaf or hard of hearing.

One formation that the Allies had little information on was *Kampfgruppe* Karst. It is not clear whether the half-tracks, armoured cars and light armour had been identified and included in the armoured totals listed in Second Army's

36

Defending the east side of the Rhine, an 88 mm flak battery.

intelligence summaries but what had been missed was that its specific role was anti-airlanding. It was German tactical doctrine to drive into the heart of an airborne drop, seeking to disrupt the enemy while he was at his most vulnerable i.e. before he could assemble and receive all of his heavier weapons. *Kampfgruppe* Karst was located to the east of the River Issel; exactly where Schlemm had assessed the Allies would deploy their airborne forces. Even though they were, in the event, just the wrong side of the Issel they were well placed to be in operation against the Allies promptly.

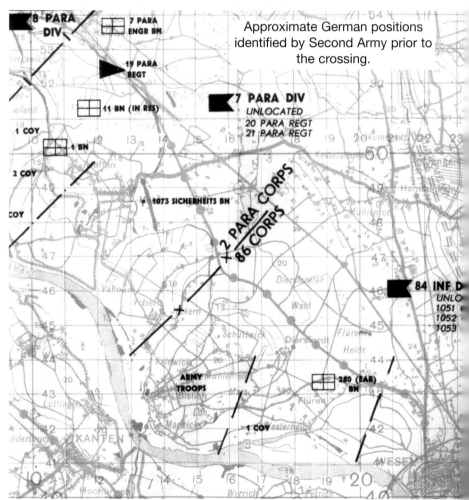

Approximate German positions identified by Second Army prior to the crossing.

When studying the operation in January 1945, Second British Army expected to face up to 58,000 German troops, with 16,000 infantry occupying defensive positions on the river line, within the assault area. It was assumed that while the Germans stood and fought west of the Rhine, that they would be bound to be preparing defences to protect the northern flank of the vital Ruhr, which Allied intelligence believed would in due course be occupied by enemy forces withdrawing east of the river. There are no firm numbers but following the German losses during VERITABLE, there can have been fewer than 7,000 infantry of a lower quality than expected dug in on the banks of the Rhine in the crossing area.

Flak was the one weapon system that the Germans had positioned along the Rhine in relative abundance, as they were expecting an airborne operation in support of an assault crossing. Deployed in and around Second Army's PLUNDER battle area were 114 heavy and 712 light anti-aircraft guns. As we will see, the abundance of flak and its effect on the battle is an indication of what could have happened on a much larger scale, if Hitler had not decided to fight west of the Rhine.

The **accompanying map** shows that even after the operation few elements of the enemy ground defence had been accurately located. This was because intelligence was limited to air photography, electronic intelligence and artillery sound ranging and without an active SOE network or a resistance organisation to pass on ground information, units in buildings and woods were difficult to identify. In addition, the *ad hoc* nature of the German defence made it difficult for intelligence officers to construct a meaningful picture of the German Order of Battle. A Royal Engineer post action report on the tactical deployment of the enemy they encountered reads:

> *Enemy ground defences in the area of the proposed crossing were not highly developed. In the main they were directed towards the protection of likely crossing points, larger villages and towns, and there was no continuous defensive line along the river. Defences mainly consisted of field positions defended buildings, all with little wire and few mines. However, where possible the Germans had flooded areas sufficiently well to make them obstacles to armour or at least very difficult going. There was little depth in the German defences.*

However, fearing the worst, the Allies were forced to prepare

**General Walter Blumentritt.**

plans for a deliberate assault crossing of the Rhine based on the fact that troops during an amphibious operation would be extremely vulnerable and that on balance the situation would favour the German defenders. In addition, they fully appreciated the German ability to mount effective counter-attacks with *ad hoc* forces and understood that it was a dangerous part of the German operational art. As with the Normandy D Day, the Allies would need to apply superior numbers, an integrated fire plan from the ground and from the air, special equipment and well-prepared troops were needed to ensure that the enemy were overcome with certainty. However, the prize was great; a firm bridgehead would provide a springboard for 21st Army Group's drive into the heart of Germany.

On 21 March, the Germans suffered another blow, when the redoubtable General Schlemm's headquarters of *First Fallschirmjäger Armie* was located by Allied intelligence. In the resulting air strike, Schlemm was badly wounded. The general called forward to take his place was General Walter Blumentritt who had been von Rundstedt's chief of staff and following his erstwhile commander's final dismissal, was now available for re-employment.

# CHAPTER THREE

# Planning and Preparation

*'... one more great campaign, aggressively conducted on a broad
front, that will give the death blow to Hitler's Germany'*
General Eisenhower

THOUGH OFTEN DISMISSED by the likes of Patton, as '...
more of a politician than a general', Eisenhower maintained a
focus on his aim; the elimination of the Ruhr as 'the heart of
continued German war fighting'. As originally intended, he
planned that the main Anglo American effort was to be in the
north under the command of the master of the deliberate attack;
Montgomery. With what he was confident would be an assured
crossing north of the Ruhr, Eisenhower justifiably believed that
further south, the other US Armies would be able to 'bounce the
Rhine'. The Supreme Commander was in effect playing to the
strengths and qualities of his Army Group and Army
commanders and the soldiers under their command.

With the Allies having reached the Rhine, there was to be no
single thrust across the great river but a series of attempts to
cross the Rhine, on a broad front, before launching the final
offensive from the resulting bridgeheads into the heart of
Germany.

Planning for the crossing and final campaign began well
before the New Year but during January and into February, the
winter weather applied a significant brake on Allied
preparation and the conduct of preliminary operations to clear
the Germans west of the Rhine.

In Operation PLUNDER, with the Ninth US Army still under
command of Montgomery's 21st Army Group, a force of British,
American and Canadians would carry out a deliberate assault
crossing of the Rhine north of the Ruhr. Completing the
envelopment of the Ruhr from the south would be First US
Army who had already captured the bridge at Remagen and
established a bridgehead.

While General Crerar's First Canadian Army was fighting
the Battle of the Rhineland, Montgomery tasked General
Dempsey's uncommitted Second Army HQ to prepare a

**General Harry Crerar talking to officers of the Queen's Own Rifles of Canada.**

deliberate crossing of the river with overwhelming numbers and overwhelming resources. By early February a planning study of the tasks involved in an assault crossing of the Rhine had been produced by the Army staff. This study was sub-divided into the four major parts: 'The assumptions on which the subsequent corps study was to be based on, intelligence, problems relating to the crossing, engineer tasks and maintenance (logistic) problems'. With this ground work established, the task of conducting a corps study and developing the assault method was allocated to XII Corps who had been relieved of operational tasks and moved to an approximately similar piece of terrain on the River Maas south of Maastricht.

When XII Corps started work 'no decision had then been taken as to whether the assault should be on a one or two corps front, but it was appreciated that if a second corps was required for the assault it could draw on XII Corps' experiences and so formulate its plans more quickly'.

### Ground

An essential prerequisite of any military planning process is to look at the topography. Considerable data was made available from a wide variety of sources, regarding the Rhine's flood plain, the flood dykes, the approaches to the river banks, the

42

average water level and sundry other detail necessary to prepare a plan. A short summary of this information is taken from the Second Army post operational report.

*The Emmerich-Wesel area lies east of the Rhine Plain, which is a five to ten miles wide, flat and rather featureless area. Water meadows extend on both sides of the river and the land closely resembles the Dutch Polder areas. To prevent flooding, there are two types of dykes:*

*1. Summer dykes, which are low dykes constructed close to the river banks to retain any normal rise in water level.*

*2. Winter dykes, which are considerably larger and built at a greater distance from the river bank. Their purpose is to retain the abnormal flooding which sometimes occurs in the Lower Rhine plains during the winter and early spring.*

*During the winter 1944–1945 the water level of the river rose to abnormal heights. All the low-lying polders within the area enclosed by the winter dykes were flooded. In addition, large areas of low-lying ground outside the winter dykes were water-logged owing to the exceptionally heavy rainfall.*

*There are numerous branches of the Alter Rhine* [old courses of the river] *in the area and there is a double water obstacle between Emmerich and Rees. The one commanding feature in the area lies to the north west of Wesel and is on the west side of the Emmerich–Wesel railway. Here the ground rises to a height of about 150 ft, is rather heavily wooded, and the area is known as the Diersfordterwald.*

The river in this sector was on average 200 yards wide, with certain sectors being up to 300 yards. The current flowed at an

**The Germans' view across the Rhine in the area of Rees. Their view was obscured by a dyke on the opposite bank, preventing them observing activity.**

Dyke

**SITE - GRAVESEND. M.R. E 059314.**

Dykes

To REES

79 ASLT SQN
RE

GRAVESEND
FERRY SITE

HOME BANK

An air reconnaissance photograph of the Rhine west of Rees, where one of the RE ferry sites was to be established once the infantry had secured the bridgehead.

44

average speed of three knots opposite Wesel. At its narrowest this stretch of the Rhine was twice the width of the point where Patton had successfully sneaked across on the night of 22/23 March 1945 and an altogether more challenging obstacle. While British and American engineers were able to examine the home bank and select entry points into the river, there was a degree of uncertainty about the state of the bank on the far side and its suitability for amphibious armour.

## Resources

As 21st Army Group was Eisenhower's main effort, allocation of logistic resources, in contrast to the MARKET GARDEN campaign, was generous enough not only to be able to get across a heavily defended strategic barrier of the Rhine but to take the battle into the heart of Germany. Eisenhower, during the planning phase, envisaged that 21st Army Group would strike east 'from the Lower Rhine north of the Ruhr and into the North German Plain' because this route offered the most suitable terrain for mobile operations ... [and] ... the quickest means of denying the Germans the vital Ruhr industries'.

Material and stores of all natures flowed into the newly opened Number 10 Army Road Head, which was sited in the wrecked country of the former Operation VERITABLE battle area. Second Army's report explained:

> From the administrative point of view, the build up of the colossal tonnages of ammunition and engineer stores presented an even greater difficulty. The only access to the area between the rivers [Maas and Rhine] lay through First Canadian Army area and over the extremely poor road system about the Reichswald Forest. This system was already cracking under the strain of the constant stream of fighting and administrative units passing over it as First Canadian Army extended its operations south east.

> In addition, Goch was a road centre vital to Second Army. Around it a large part of the administrative layout revolved, it was about this very point that the Germans had decided to hold.

> A plan had been made to govern the priority of road development up to and forward of the R Maas ... based on the construction of [five] bridges from north to south as the Canadian advance progressed. This bridging task was given to Second Army.

The reality of living in the battle-wrecked country was explained by Brigadier Essame: 'at the end of the second week of March the weather suddenly changed to spring.'

*Leaving the 3rd and 52nd Lowland Divisions to hold the line of the Rhine the rest of the assault troops of 21st Army Group pulled back to the ground over which they fought in the mud and sleet of winter. There were mines and wire everywhere ... Not a single house had escaped utter ruin... dirty straw, broken ammunition boxes, empty tins, the garbage of two armies fouled the ground.*

Into this area troops poured, not only to establish the logistic infrastructure but for training as well. Massive traffic circuits and dumps were laid out. The scale of the preparations is hard to grasp; 30,000 tons of engineer material was piled for miles along the road north from Goch, with an additional tonnage pre-loaded on 940 vehicles. 60,000 tons of ammunition, were stacked along ten miles of the north south road just east of the Maas and 28,000 tons of combat supplies were dumped around the ruined town of Kevlaer, its rubble being used to create areas of hard standing. All of this work required huge manpower resources. All available Pioneer Corps companies were involved in establishing the supply dumps, while twelve battalions of US Engineers were loaned to 21st Army Group to build bridges and maintain the crumbling country roads, whose builders had not intended them for sustained heavy military traffic. Including those training for the assault crossing, there were about 60,000 engineers involved in PLUNDER in a wide variety of capacities. To these should be added Dutch and Belgian civilians working to repair the infrastructure in their own countries.

The build up and preparation presented very real problems of camouflage and concealment that were considered by HQ Second Army to be 'somewhat similar to those met in the UK before Operation Neptune', except that German patrols were crossing the river looking for evidence of the dumping of bridging stores and other preparations on the home bank. Second Army reported that 'The planners accepted that it was impossible to conceal from the enemy the fact that 21st Army Group intended to assault the Rhine north of the Ruhr, but great care was taken to ensure that the date and place of assault were not prejudiced'. This statement is at odds with the efforts made by the logistic planners and Royal Engineers' camouflage

**Pioneers laying a log road in one of the forests that was to hide the thousands of men and vehicles that were to take part in Operation PLUNDER.**

companies to disguise the growing stacks of stores. Typically, they would be piled in linear dumps along roadsides not only for easy access but also so that to a recce aircraft, they would resemble hedgerows. Similarly dumps would be established in and around villages where they could be camouflaged as buildings. The historian of 94th Field Regiment RA recorded

**LVT crews 'camming-up' in a wood prior to PLUNDER.**

how 'recce parties went forward individually towards the banks of the river to select their gun positions without attracting attention' and how when they finally occupied these gun positions on 22 March:

> *Most strict orders had been issued that the guns, tractors, ammunition and everything must be completely invisible when daylight came, and daylight did reveal a masterpiece of camouflage.*

This view was confirmed by an RAF recce sortie that was launched on D-1 to check for evidence that would lead German aircraft and photo interpreters to identify the location of the coming assault.

### 21st Army Group Plan

For Operation PLUNDER, 21st Army Group comprised three armies; Ninth US Army, Second British Army and First Canadian Army. The assaults by Second and Ninth Armies would be launched simultaneously.

The task of Ninth United States Army was, to mount an assault crossing of the Rhine in the area of Rheinberg and to secure a bridgehead from the junction of the Ruhr and Rhine rivers to Bottrop and Dorsten. Thereafter, General Simpson was to be prepared to advance to a general line inclusive of Hamm and Munster. Ninth US Army's tasks also included the protection of the right flank of Second British Army and the vital bridging sites at Wesel.

Second British Army was to assault the Rhine in the area of Xanten and Rees and to establish a bridgehead between Rees and Wesel and subsequently advance on a three corps front north east towards the town of Rheine.

Initially the task of First Canadian Army was to assist in

**The Army Commander's pennant from General Crerar's Jeep.**

broadening the frontage of Second Army's assault by carrying out feint attacks along the Rhine on their left flank, while holding securely the line of the rivers Rhine and Maas from Emmerich westwards to the sea. The Canadians were, however, represented in the assault phase by 9th Canadian Infantry Brigade. Made up of Canadian highland battalions, such as the Stormont, Dundas

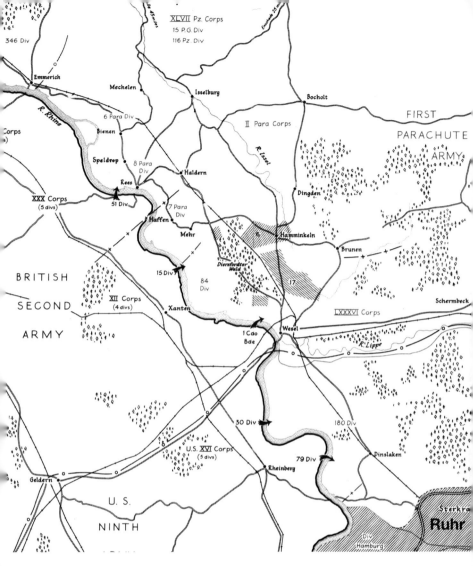

and Glengarry Highlanders were attached to 51st Highland Division, as its fourth brigade. Later First Canadian Army was to be prepared to advance into eastern Holland and to protect the left flank of Second Army. The story of the Ninth US Army and 17th US Airborne Division is contained in the **Battleground** title *US Rhine Crossing* by Andrew Rawson.

## Air Operations
With some difficulty the bomber barons were prevailed upon to coordinate their activities with those of the Army. The air forces

would have rather continued to concentrate on the 'Thunderclap Plan', which was designed to deliver a sudden and catastrophic blow by bombing Berlin, Dresden, Chemnitz and Leipzig, with a view to bringing about Germany's surrender. The support needed by the ground forces required the bomber commanders to carry out a comprehensive programme of interdiction sorties in support of PLUNDER; the 'Ruhr Plan'. Ninth Tactical Air Force planned to isolate the area north of the Ruhr and prevent the movement of German reserves to the battlefield. As the three railway lines in the area had already been heavily bombed, it would, therefore, concentrate on sixteen significant bridges giving access to the battle area. However, as a part of their attempt to bomb Germany into submission, the air forces tripled the tonnage of bombs the Armies requested, with the result that the final advance across northern Germany was often slowed by the results of earlier bomber sorties.

## Second British Army's Plan

After much study the plan that was eventually arrived at, called for an assault on a frontage of two corps (XII and XXX Corps), with a planned D Day being the night of 23/24 March 1945. In outline, the plan made by General Dempsey, commander Second Army, was to assault with two corps:

*RIGHT XII Corps, LEFT XXX Corps, each with one division up. VIII Corps was to hold securely the West bank of the R RHINE during the concentration period until the assault corps were ready to assume control of divisions holding the river line immediately before the assault.*

*XVIII US Airborne Corps was to be dropped east of the R RHINE after the river assaults had taken place. The principles for its employment were that it should drop within range of artillery sited on the West bank of the R RHINE and that the link up with the ground forces should take place on D Day.*

*To release Headquarters XVIII US Airborne Corps as soon as possible, Headquarters 8 Corps was to take over from that corps within seven days.*

*Second Army would then be correctly positioned to continue the advance into the North German plains with 8 Corps RIGHT, 12 Corps CENTRE and 30 Corps LEFT.*

*II Canadian Corps was to be passed through the LEFT of*

*Second Army bridgehead and handed back to First Canadian
Army when it was in a position to exercise command.*

In the **first phase** of Second Army's plan, the two assault
divisions were to capture the low-lying ground east of the river
up to approximately the line of the Wesel–Emmrich railway.
XXX Corps would begin the attack on the left flank, astride
Rees, at 2100 hours on 23 March, with 1 Commando Brigade
crossing the Rhine to seize Wesel an hour later, while XII Corps
would be led by 15th Scottish Division's assault from the area of
Xanten at 0200 hours. At the same time, XVI US Corps would
launch their attack south of Wesel.

The **second phase** was to be the capture of the
Issel bridges, with or without the assistance of
XVIII US Airborne Corps (Operation VARSITY –
scheduled for 1000 hours on 24 March), as they
could easily be prevented from dropping by poor
weather. By the time they launched the assault,
Second Army were confident that they could,
indeed capture the bridges unaided if necessary,
albeit in slower time and with greater casualties.

In contrast with MARKET GARDEN where
three airborne divisions had been dropped over
several days up to sixty miles from the front line,
XVII US Corps's drop and landing zones were
concentrated between just three and six miles

**Shoulder flash of XVIII
US Airborne Corps.**

from the Rhine, well within the range of Second Army's
medium guns. In addition, the airborne divisions, in Operation
VARSITY, were not to be committed until a viable bridgehead
across the Rhine had been formed by the US and British infantry
Divisions (operations TURNSCREW, TORCHLIGHT and
FLASHLIGHT). In short, the inadequacies and over ambitious
planning assumptions of MARKET GARDEN were not to be
repeated.

Landing in daylight, in a single wave, in over just three
hours, the two divisions were to seize vital villages, the wooded
Diersfordter feature and capture the crossings of the River Issel,
necessary for a swift breakout from the Rhine Bridgehead.

The breakout on to the North German Plain would be **Phase
Three** of the operation.

With the fighting on the west bank of the Rhine only having
finally ended on 11 March there were less than two weeks to

**G Wing of 79 Armoured Division developing assault techniques on the Maas River.**

complete the planning, deployment and implementation of the largest and most complex amphibious and airborne operation since the Normandy landings. This was a tall order but after nine months of campaigning the British and Canadian formation staffs were up to the challenge.

## Training

Having taken part in the first half of Operation VERITABLE, 15th Scottish Division was selected to lead the assault across the Rhine and on the 26th February they were withdrawn and

**A carpet-laying amphibious Buffalo or Landing Vehicle Tracked (LVT) practising for its role of improving the exits across the river mud.**

**The amphibious LVT climbing a river bank to land its cargo of troops 'dry-shod' some distance inland.**

placed under XII Corps on the River Maas for the purposes of developing techniques and for training. Grouped with the Corps was G Wing of 79th Armoured Division ('Hobart's Funnies'), who had in the meantime, been working on developing or adapting amphibious equipment and tactical doctrine for river crossings. With the following additions, General Hobart's command became, at 21,430 men, easily the largest division in the British Army. In January, 33 Armoured Brigade joined leaving behind their Sherman tanks and retraining on the amphibious Buffalo or as it was officially known, the Landing Vehicle Tracked (LVT). The Staffordshire Yeomanry and 44 Royal Tank Regiment under HQ 4th Armoured Brigade joined the division to train with DD tanks. Lieutenant Colonel Hopkinson, Commanding Officer 44 RTR wrote:

> *Yes it was all too true, we the 44th Royal Tank Regiment had joined the Wavy Navy and were to sail our way across the Rhine in the same type of DD tanks with inflatable skirts as were used*

*for the amphibious landings on D-Day. Then ensued a furious period of training – 10 days – from morning to night. Nautical terms were freely used!*

This training and preparation along with other innovations, including radio beacons and shaded lights for navigation on the river in darkness or smoke, carpet laying versions of the Buffalo to create exits over soft mud and RE heavy rafts, all helped ensure success.

When it became apparent that XXX Corps was also going to be carrying out an assault crossing 51st Highland Division were extracted from the battle and went through a similar package of training exercises based on the doctrine developed by XII Corps and 15th and 79th Divisions. Lieutenant Campbell of 5 Black Watch commented of one preparatory exercise:

*We hadn't seen the Buffaloes before and we hadn't had much practice in the dark. In the fog, we got turned around and landed downstream on the same side we started from.*

It is worth noting that thirty-six of the Royal Navy's Landing Craft Vehicle (Personnel) (LCV(P)) and a similar number of Mark 3 Landing Craft Mechanised (LCM) were brought to the Rhine. Lieutenant Peter White of 4 KOSB recalled watching the

**Royal Navy landing craft on its way inland to the Rhine.**

build-up of forces: '...we were astonished to see even Royal Navy involved. Enormous transporters lumbered by, with sailors and marines and assorted craft aboard, some as big as 45 feet long and 14 feet broad which had been hauled overland through Holland and Belgium.'

Known as Force U, under command of Captain James RN, the landing craft had been intended to carry troops and equipment across the Rhine early in the assault. So successful had XII Corps and 79th Division been in their work that, in the event, the craft were relegated to more mundane but none the less important tasks on the river, principally in support of the Royal Engineers.

Also training on the Maas was 1 Commando Brigade, still under former Guardsman, Brigadier Derek Mills-Roberts, who had taken over command when Lord Lovat had been wounded in Normandy. The Brigade commander believed in thorough training and would have his units repeat exercises until they were perfect, all the while with the incentive of time off for those who got it right more quickly. He was also determined to minimise casualties and took measures to ensure that his men would not suffer for the want of resources and that casualties would be promptly evacuated. Problems identified during training were resolved and mitigating measures built into his emerging plan.

### Preparations

Lieutenant Douglas Goddard of 112 Field Regiment RA, having fought throughout VERITABLE, recorded details of that other necessary pre-operational requirement; rest.

**Lieutenant Douglas Goddard.**

*The nine days rest period since the end of Veritable, spent at Bergen, was occupied with catching up on baths, sorting out personal kit and battery equipment, absorbing and inducting reinforcements and of course training. It was also the opportunity to take in an ENSA concert or see a film or two.*

While many of the combat troops were resting, training or briefing, the services were working to gather all possible resources to support the assault, which was to be the last great set piece

55

battle of the war. Corporal Douglas Robinson, of 297 Company RASC, whose DUKWs had originally been a part of the beach group working on Juno Beach, and had been invaluable in coping with the Rhine Floods during VERITABLE was sent to help the effort.

*On 18 March we came under the command of the Second British Army and moved to Bonninghardt, from where we were transporting 25-pounder shells and petrol from Nijmegen to the small village of Werrich ..., where all the stores were stockpiled along the hedgerows, together with the tanks and guns, in readiness for the Rhine crossing, our last load of four tons of ammunition was left on the DUKW.*

**Corporal Douglas Robinson.**

Being one of the laden vehicles that was to cross the Rhine in the first two days, Corporal Robinson's DUKW was issued packet serial numbers as a part of the traffic management plan. This plan incorporated a methodology of being able to change priorities and to call forward to the crossing point the supplies or troops needed most urgently at the front.

Lieutenant Peter White of 4 KOSB, who as part of 52nd (Lowland) Division, was in the area just west of the Rhine, recalled:

*Interesting units and vehicles, including amphibious tanks and Buffaloes, bridging pontoons, hundreds of guns and mountains of ammunition, were piling into every available space. During daylight hours, more and more smoke generators and canisters tended by pioneers appeared over the countryside, pouring out coiling billows of bluish and yellow smoke screens to keep the enemy guessing on the date and place of the crossing.*

**Lieutenant Peter White.**

The smoke, designed to screen the west bank from observation from the other side of the river had been started as First Canadian Army advanced south east from the Groesbeek Heights towards Wesel. With the dyke on the far bank being higher than on the home bank, the essential

**Pioneer Corps soldiers maintain the screen on the banks of the Rhine with smoke generators.**

smoke screen was now maintained by four Pioneer Corps smoke companies to conceal the preparations. The companies were made up of no less than 1,350 men, who one old soldier described as 'ineligible for any other arm of the service, with a sprinkling of intellectuals considered to be of no military value elsewhere'. They worked under a headquarters known as Smoke Control and expended during VERITABLE and PLUNDER 8,500 zinc chloride smoke generators and about 450,000 gallons of fog oil to maintain a screen up to sixty-six miles long. Their work was when combined with smoke from the fires in Wesel, extremely effective, however, the Dakota and glider pilots carrying the airborne divisions, perhaps found their work a little too effective.

Lieutenant White continued his account of the build-up west of the Rhine:

*While taking a spin round the area, enjoying a 'liberated' motorcycle, I was struck anew at the rapidly massing material for the river crossing. ... Guns and materials speckled the landscape as thickly as it had once been sprinkled with cattle. The hedgerows were lined and the barns bursting with supplies and ammunition. Other shell dumps were camouflaged as false haystacks. Every house and farm was becoming packed with troops, among them those of the 51st Highland Division and our sister Battalion 1st KOSB. The woods were bristling with tanks, normal, amphibious with Duplex drive and other weird types for special purposes. Massed in other areas were Buffaloes and DUKW amphibious vehicles and fantastic quantities of bridging materials.*

Variously known as 'Movement Light', 'Artificial Moonlight' or even 'Monty's Moonlight' search light units were deployed into the assault area on a large scale, with the idea of reflecting light off a cloud base. Some nights prior to the assault they were used to 'accustom the Germans to their presence' and no doubt aid the deployment into forward assembly areas. The searchlight unit HQ generally referred to as 'Moonlight Ops' was tasked with adjusting the intensity of light from the River bank in accordance with requests from the commanders concerned.

If the location of the assault were to remain a secret one thing that had to be controlled was reconnaissance. Lieutenant General Horrocks, commander XXX Corps, explained:

*Before an attack of this sort a large number of people must go forward and reconnoitre the position they are to occupy. This applies particularly to the Gunners, who have many mysterious rites of their own to perform before they can bring down accurate concentrations of fire. Nobody was allowed forward on to the flat Polderland stretching back from the banks of the Rhine without reporting to a special branch of XXX Corps H.Q., where a very large-scale map of the forward area was maintained. This was known as 'The Pig Hotel'. After examining the accommodation on the map*

**Lieutenant General Horrocks wearing the 'Old Pig' of XXX Corps.**

*which they had been allocated, the reconnaissance parties were allowed to go forward a few at a time to see their 'rooms', which, if satisfactory, were then marked up on the plan as 'booked'.*

Captain Goulden of 59 GHQ Troops Engineer Regiment was

one of those who went forward to the river for a recce of the four sites where the Regiment's squadrons were to ferry troops across the Rhine:

*We decided to do a night recce on the 14th. I visited corps, division and battalions, and then went to see the company of infantry holding that particular sector of the Rhine. The CRE [Commander Royal Engineers] and I went down to the forward company and as dusk was falling we met the Company commander. As soon as it was dark enough he took us down to the forward position at the bank on the river bank where the old Rees ferry used to operate and we were introduced to the infantry patrol which was to accompany us. There was a slight mist at the time and there were vague rumours of enemy patrols on our side of the river. The whole situation was rather eerie ... and the farms were quite deserted.*

*After some time, we set out with the infantry patrol down to the water's edge where in a low mist on the water and half moonlight, as far as possible we avoided the crunchy patches of gravel. The patrol moved along about half way up the foreshore and the CRE and I worked along the edge of the water. We waded out testing the slopes of the banks on our chosen beaches and feeling the firmness of the mud. We had nearly finished the stretch of beach which we had been allotted when we were told by the infantry commander that he would rather not go any further as he was coming into the next company area. He was not sure of the stability of the nerves of his neighbours, though they had been informed that we would be out that night. So we then turned and worked our way back to the house at the ferry. After a few cheery words we were conducted back to company headquarters, to battalion and to our car.*

General Horrocks highlighted the fact that not everyone was as careful in the conduct of their recce as they should have been:

*I was particularly angry one day to hear that a certain Major General, who was much too brave to take the normal precautions, had walked along the near bank of the Rhine, wearing his red hat. He subsequently left our area, with a monumental flea in his ear.*

To facilitate commanders' daylight recces, the smoke screen was briefly allowed to disperse but on one occasion the wind changed and the commanders peering from camouflaged Observation posts built into the dykes only got a 'watery eye squint'.

Perhaps potentially the most obvious preparations were those being made by the Royal Artillery. 1,300 British and 600 US field, medium and heavy guns, their numerous vehicles and stockpiles of ammunition were difficult to conceal. So large was the number of guns to move and so few the routes available for them, it was not possible to bring the batteries forward in one move but they had to be brought up over the nights between 21 and 23 March using staging areas about six miles from the river. By the morning of 23 March, the majority of the guns were in their pre-recced forward positions. However, Captain Whately-Smith wrote: 'As one looked around it was hard to believe that these fields and orchards concealed a mass of artillery waiting in silence for the evening zero hour'.

While Second Army's preparations for the amphibious assault across the Rhine were underway, XVIII US Airborne Corps, who were to come under command of the British Second Army, were similarly making ready at their bases in the UK and France.

All that could be done, had been done. The staff had prepared meticulously for this massively complicated operation; material was stockpiled, the soldiers were ready. The scene was set for another typical Montgomery set piece battle and victory, just as Eisenhower had intended.

CHAPTER 4

# Operation TURNSCREW
# 51st Highland Division

*'Forward on wings of flame to final victory'*
Winston Churchill 23 March 1945

WITH THE WEATHER and state of the river all looking suitable for the assault crossing and airborne drop, 'At 1530 hours on 23rd March, I [Montgomery] gave orders to launch the operation...'

51st Highland Division was to lead XXX Corps' assault across the Rhine at 2100 hours on D-1. With elements of 3rd Division holding the home bank in the Corps's sector, the initial crossing was to be launched from the area from opposite the German-held town of Rees northwards. Two battalions each from 153 and 154 Brigades were to form the leading flight in what were to be the opening moves of Second British Army's largest amphibious assault operation since D-Day.

**XXX Corps (above) and 51st Highland Division.**

XXX Corps's orders for the initial phase were:

'...to capture Rees and Haldern and establish a bridgehead sufficiently deep to permit bridges to be built, preparatory to a further advance into Germany. 51 (H) Division, with under command 9 Canadian Brigade of 3 Canadian Division, was to assault and secure the initial bridgehead, 9 Canadian Brigade being committed on the LEFT flank. Immediately after, one infantry brigade and divisional headquarters of 43 (Wx) Division were to be passed across the river. 43 Division was to take 9 Canadian Brigade under command and relieve the LEFT brigade of 51 (H) Division.*

At least a part of the purpose of 51st Highland Division's preliminary assault crossing, five hours before the main effort by 15th Scottish Division, was to widen the frontage of the assault, in order to give a larger objective for the inevitable German counter-attack and to draw away German reserves from the Xanten–Wesel area. In other words, it was a classic

Montgomery move designed to unbalance the enemy before the main blow fell.

Major General Rennie's plan for 51st Highland Division was to assault with two brigades, 153 and 154. Their initial tasks were to secure the bank and objectives little more than a thousand yards inland. In the case of 153 Brigade, their second wave (1 Gordon) was to capture Rees, while that of 154 Brigade (1 Black Watch) was to expand the bridgehead by capturing the villages of Speldrop and Klein Esserden. 152 Brigade was to send a battalion (2nd Seaforth) over the river to support 153 Brigade in the capture of Rees before midnight on D-1. The remainder of 152 Brigade were to follow and further expand the bridgehead.

**Major General Rennie.**

The area chosen for the Highland Division's landing was bounded by one of the horseshoe lakes (meres) and marshy areas created when the Rhine abandoned its old course. This provided the 51st Highland Division with some protection, however, to expand northward the villages of Speldrop and Bienen had to be taken. Speldrop itself lies at the centre of the great horseshoe and Bienen at its northern end. The Germans had fully appreciated the tactical value of these places, and had prepared counter-attacks which they could launch promptly.

In the area that 153 Brigade were to assault, the cover from view and fire offered to the enemy by the small riverside town of Rees was exploited to the full and was known to be occupied by elements of 8th *Fallschirmjäger* Division. Positioned amongst the buildings on the river's edge, the determined *Fallschirmjäger* were able to dominate potential crossing points astride the town and the flood plains, especially that immediately to the east. Artillery observers had good positions of observation from Rees Cathedral and mill tower across the whole area. As Lieutenant

General Horrocks was to bemoan, XXX Corps's '...bad luck that once more we should be faced by these diehard Nazis ... we heard stories, from US and our flanking corps, of German soldiers surrendering in their thousands ... while we had to fight hard right up to the end'.

*Generalmajor* Miendel, commander *II Fallschirmjäger Korps.*

### Final Preparations and the Bombardment
Assembly and thorough briefing of the force, was one of Montgomery's prerequisites for success and the few troops who

Sappers prepare the carpet that their LVT will use to create an exit from the river.

A British 5.5 inch medium gun in action at night.

took part recall more comprehensive briefings since those during the run-up to D Day. As already recorded, the assault troops had moved into their forward assembly areas in the woods and valleys, three miles west of the Rhine, all being in position early on 23 March (D-1). Here they slept, waited and carried out their battle preparations; last letters were written, radios, other specialist equipment, weapons and ammunition were checked and cleaned and life jackets fitted. Company commanders read Montgomery's message to their soldiers, while quartermaster sergeants brought up hot food, the last to be seen for some time and finally faces were blackened.

The first troops to move down through the units holding the Rhine to the river bank were the Royal Engineers. As night fell, at 2000hrs 3rd Division's Sappers started work on creating gaps through the dykes and ramps down into the river. Behind them, other sappers, including 50 GHQ Engineers, began to build roads, such as that which became known as Caledonian Road, across the flood plain to the gap in the bank. In maintaining and improving the gap the Royal Engineers 'were subject to almost continuous, and at times heavy, enemy shell, mortar and machine gun fire throughout the night and some forty-five casualties were caused'. Despite the attentions of the enemy, several lengths of road up to 800 yards long were successfully laid during the night of 23/24 March.

Finally, in darkness, the time came and, around 2030 hours, as described in Second Army's history, the

*'... assault formations slipped out of their hides and turned their LVTs towards the east. Across the broad floodplain toward the dark swift-running waters of the great barrier of the R Rhine amphibians picked their careful paths, assisted by movement light. A tremendous artillery barrage roared encouragement. The curtain had risen on the opening phases of the last battle of the European war'.*

As there was little chance of forming up on the riverbank without being detected by the enemy, the assault force were all mounted in LVTs and, with the DD tanks of the Staffordshire Yeomanry following, motored down to their crossing points on pre-recced routes. Covering the sound of movement and softening up the 8th *Fallschirmjäger* Division, who were dug-in on the far bank, was the bombardment that had begun at 1700 hours and by 2100 hours, it was being fired by all the available guns of 21st Army Group. This was the beginning of what was reckoned to be the greatest British artillery bombardment of the war being fired by some 5,500 guns. 112 Field Regiment, for example had to take part in firing two fireplans codenamed 'Snifter' and 'Sherry' and a 'milk round' of counter battery tasks all against identified enemy gun and mortar positions. Just before H Hour, other regiments engaged some of the areas on the opposite bank with the aim of detonating enemy landmines.

Major Martin Lindsay of 1 Gordons, recalled that:

> *'There was a continuous ripple of slams and bangs as all our guns, stretching across so many fields behind, were firing, and it went on for four hours ... meanwhile quite a lot of stuff was beginning to come back from the other side, mostly medium and light mortars. One mortar in particular was dropping its bombs all round this house. At 7.30 p.m., there was still one and a half hours to go. A tremendous rumble of guns behind us, their shells whistling overhead, and the nice sharp banging sound of our 25-pounders landing on the far bank.'*

Lieutenant Beck, Gun Position Officer of B Troop, 341 Battery, 86th Field Regt RA (Herts Yeomanry) recorded in the battery command post log that not all went well for the gunners:

> *'The operation began with the roar of massed guns at zero*

**LVTs making their way down to the river in the fading light and smoke.**

*hour and the firing continued all night. Bofors, mortars and rocket guns all joined in and the air was alive with tracer shells being pumped into the defences on the opposite bank. Soon after midnight, an unfortunate accident occurred on D Sub of A Troop. No one will ever know what happened but it would seem that in loading the gun in the dark the loader accidentally hit the shell fuse against the breech. Normally this would not cause an accident but the fuse must have been faulty. The shell exploded killing instantly the occupants of the compartment ... it was a grim reminder that the shells the gunners handled so easily were lethal. We had become so accustomed to them that we had almost ruled out the possibility of danger, the safety devices were known to be foolproof.*

### The Assault Crossing

Mounted in 150 amphibious Buffaloes, with one troop of four LVTs per infantry company and attached personnel, the leading four infantry battalions of 51st Highland Division reached the final holding area. The nucleus of the Bank Control Group was provided by the Royal Dragoons, dismounted from their tanks for the task. This unglamorous but absolutely vital job, according to Corps Commander, General Horrocks, '... was no easy task, as units had to be marshalled into their correct area and/or lanes in the dark, while all moves were coordinated with extreme accuracy'.

Captain Stafford of 617 Assault Squadron RE, who were to establish a ferry near Mahnenburg once the initial crossing had been made recalled:

*The great night of 23 March arrived and I with my troop sergeant, loaded up the scout car with recce equipment and, at 1800 hours, we moved up to the forward assembly area of 1 BW, with whom we were to cross the river that night. We arranged to lie in hiding in Honnoppel until H Hour..., and then to proceed to the LVT loading point 400 yards behind the flood bank, where we were to get a lift across the river* [as a part of the second wave].

*The period between 1900 and 2100 hours was one which I'll never forget. Every gun in the area was taking part in a most terrific barrage and at times I thought our machine guns might have done well to raise their fire a few feet higher, as the tracer seemed dangerously close. By 2100 hrs, the barrage reached its peak, and the assault wave left the home bank.*

Through the gaps and into the water went the LVTs. Cpl James Campbell of 7 Argyle & Sutherland Highlanders recalled the four minute trip across the river in the Buffalo:

*We got into our Buffaloes and ran down to the river, with the artificial moonlight going – that is searchlights shining on the cloud base and reflecting back down on the water – all you could hear was people shouting "turn these so and so lights off" because we felt that we were silhouetted on the river and if we could see two or three hundred yards up and down the river then so could the Germans see us sat out in the middle like ducks.*

*There was quite a bit of machine-gun fire from the German side of the River. Although we had a point 5 calibre machine gun on the Buffalo we were only too glad to be out of the river and across the other side.*

Trooper Walter Fuller of 4 RTR recalled:

*For this operation our Shermans had been replaced with American Buffalo amphibious tanks, supporting the 51st Highland Division. It was pitch black as we led our tanks into the water, we couldn't see and had no idea what to expect, other than that being the first unit over the Rhine no doubt meant resistance would be heavy. It was an extremely nerve-wracking crossing, especially as we had only just changed over from the Shermans we were used to! After a while though we realised that in fact there was next to no resistance and our crossing was all but uncontested, which was a huge relief. When we reached the other side I remember one man, Colonel Alan Jolly [CO 4 RTR], planting the regimental flag on the eastern bank of the river. It was in fact the very same flag taken into battle by the unit in the First World War and was a proud moment for us all.*

While for most things went well during the crossing of the first wave, but for Bill Robertson of 154 Brigade things looked difficult for a time.

*My most vivid memory of WWII was crossing the Rhine ...1945, four days after my 19th birthday ... in amphibious vehicles called Buffaloes which were run by the*

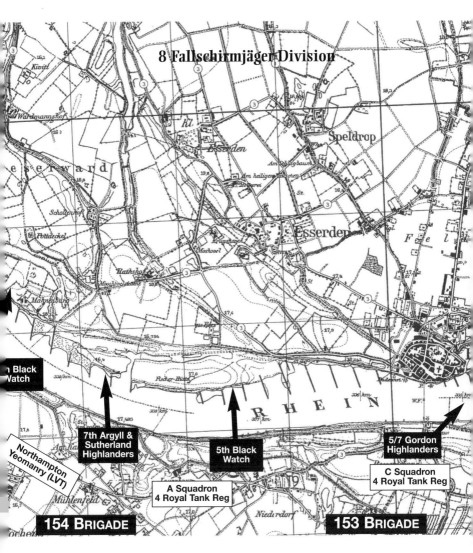

**8 Fallschirmjäger Division**

Speldrop

Esserden

154 BRIGADE

153 BRIGADE

Black Watch

7th Argyll & Sutherland Highlanders

Northampton Yeomanry (LVT)

5th Black Watch

A Squadron 4 Royal Tank Reg

5/7 Gordon Highlanders

C Squadron 4 Royal Tank Reg

RHEIN

*Northamptonshire Yeomanry. We were half way across when our tracks locked and we went around in a circle and drifted. We all thought we were going to have to jump or swim for it, but at the last minute the tracks started up again.*

General Horrocks, accompanied by his tactical HQ, with little else to do at this point in the battle, had climbed into an observation post on some high ground overlooking the Rhine. He recalled that 'All around me were the usual noises of battle but I could see very little except the flicker of the guns'. Horrocks, however, did not have to wait long before, at 2117 hours, he received the message timed at 2104 'The Black Watch has landed safely on the far bank'.

## 154 Brigade

The task given to Brigadier James Oliver was to form a bridgehead a mile and a half deep, to the east of Rees, including the villages of Klein Esserden (not to be confused with Esserden which was in 153 Brigade's area) and Speldrop. The assault was to be led by two battalions, 7 Black Watch and 7 Argyls, with the third battalion, 1 Black Watch, crossing into the bridgehead later.

7 Black Watch (first to report their landing and suffer casualties) and 7 Argylls and Sutherland Highlanders, crossing on the Division's left, climbed up the steep banks, out of the river in their tracked amphibians with a little difficulty, astride Mahnenburg. One of the Northamptonshire Yeomanry's LVT was knocked out by a *Teller-mine*, on the enemy bank. While 7 Black Watch were debussing from their Buffaloes, further casualties were sustained from anti-personnel *Schumines* that had been scattered thinly along the banks. Accompanying the infantry were engineers of 274 Field Company, whose task was to clear the bank of mines before the arrival of the subsequent waves, as well as helping construct exit ramps to ease their passage.

C Company 7 Black Watch secured their battalion's bridgehead, while B Company advanced on Potdeckel. Once secure A Company set off to their objective of Scholtenhof, further inland. Lieutenant Colonel Cathcart's Tactical HQ was established in Potdeckel with B Company. D Company then advanced between A and B to complete the battalion's initial objectives and took the hamlet of Wardmannshof, with the assistance of two Wasp flame-throwers. C Company remained in reserve, securing the bank for subsequent waves. By dawn the 'Black Jocks' had coordinated their defensive positions and were digging-in, with detachments of medium machine gunners from 1/7 Middlesex, in time to beat off a *Fallschirmjäger* counter-attack that was launched under cover of the early morning mist.

Meanwhile, 7 Argyll and Sutherland Highlanders after an

uneventful crossing in the Buffaloes of the Nottinghamshire Yeomanry, who had landed the battalion exactly as intended, set about executing their plan, which Captain Ian Cameron

An early version of the Wasp flame-thrower conversion of the Bren gun carrier, issued to infantry battalions with two tanks holding a total of 100 gallons of flame fuel.

recalled:

*The plan for the 7th Argylls was to attack with A Company forward on the right and B Company on their left, with D Company following up behind A company. A Company were to make for Ratshoff, which was a small village, and B Company were to make for a farm a bit to the left of this. D Company were then to go through A Company and make for a crossroads beyond Ratshoff.*

On reaching the enemy

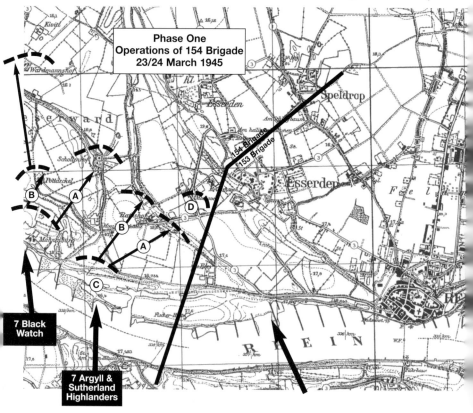

Phase One
Operations of 154 Brigade
23/24 March 1945

154 Brigade

153 Brigade

7 Black Watch

7 Argyll & Sutherland Highlanders

154 BRIGADE

153 BRIGADE

bank, 'the cordite and smoke from the creeping barrage was hanging low over the area and the general atmosphere resembled a London fog'. It was only a matter of minutes before the companies found their bearings and set off towards their objectives around Ratshoff and the crossroads beyond. 'The first phase went according to plan, and all companies captured their objectives quickly against light opposition, along with about 100 prisoners.'

Thus, the initial phase of 154 Brigade's part in the operation had been completed remarkably smoothly, against *Fallschirmjäger*, who were thinly spread and still stunned by the tremendous bombardment. Well before dawn, the leading battalions were digging-in to form a firm bridgehead. The Brigade's reserve battalion 1 Black Watch was crossing and moving up to expand the bridgehead in the Brigade's second phase.

At 2100 hours Black Watch was forming up in the assembly area awaiting the return of the Buffaloes from the river. Crossing with the Black Watch was Captain Stafford and his RE recce party.

*My troop sergeant and I left our scout car and walked off, loaded with a wireless set, mine detectors, prodders, tracing tape, numerous small hand lamps, etc, to the LVT loading point. After a short walk, we boarded a Buffalo, sat on top of a small armoured car, up went the ramp and off we went for our short 'swim', I might add that up to this time enemy fire had been negligible, but the sky was lit up by a chandelier type of flare which, made me feel most conspicuous.*

1 Black Watch touched down on the far bank just after 2300 hours and passing through 7 Argylls, made for the villages of Speldrop and Klein Esserden. They soon ran into trouble; and Major Richard Boyle was killed leading B Company on the approaches to Klein Esserden, which according to the Battalion's post operational report '... was a strong position of houses and deep minefields, resolutely defended by parachutists'. To make matters worse and deny crucial fire support, the artillery observation officer's carrier and his radio were destroyed by a mine. The battalion was now unable to contact the artillery back on the home bank and could not adjust fire, which would normally deliver a crushing blow to the enemy before the infantry's final assault. With heavy enemy

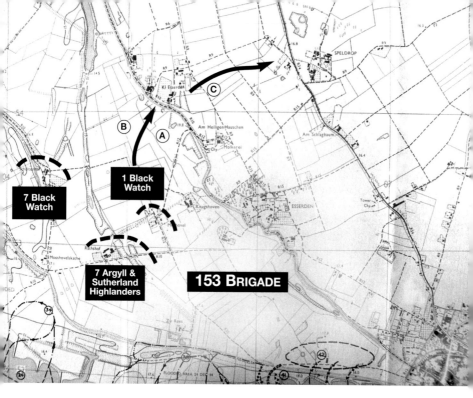

mortar fire directed at them, 1 Black Watch was suffering casualties. However, virtually unsupported, A Company took the Creamery on the outskirts of the village without much difficulty and B Company, with only one officer left unwounded, went on to occupy the main part of Klein Esserden. C Company advanced on Speldrop a thousand yards away. In reaching Speldrop they had succeeded in isolating Rees from the north west, thus protecting the left flank and 1 Gordons (153 Brigade) who would be attacking Rees from the west, from start lines behind the Black Watch.

By 0600 hours, the Commanding Officer, Lieutenant Colonel Hopwood was reporting, from his Tac HQ, now established in the Klein Esserden creamery, back to Brigade HQ that he had moved forward from the river bank and that

**The view from the river dyke inland to Esserden over the country to be crossed by 5 Black Watch.**

his companies had taken their objectives. The Black Watch had far more of a fight against *Fallschirmjäger* who had the opportunity to recover from the bombardment, as well as benefiting from the support of immediate reserves. To make matters worse there were soon disturbing reports that C Company in Speldrop were under mounting pressure from *Fallschirmjäger* counter-attacks.

Under darkness and mist, a very heavy enemy counter-attack had infiltrated into Speldrop and C Company, who were fighting in the buildings, which they had not had time to prepare for defence were forced to give ground. In addition, their 'bag of sixty German prisoners had already to be set free'. Such was the danger of the company being overwhelmed and Colonel Hopwood decided to withdraw them at 0800 hours and subsequently B Company were also forced back. Both companies were brought in behind A Company in the area of the Creamery. One platoon of C Company was, however, isolated and could not pull back with the rest of the company.

Lieutenant Robert Henderson, a nineteen-year-old subaltern, volunteered to go out with a fighting patrol to attempt to extricate the lost platoon. Advancing along a hedgerow his

**The loose straggle village of Speldrop from Klein Esserden.**

patrol came under intense *Spandau* fire. Virtually pinned down, Lieutenant Henderson ordered his men to remain in cover; along with a Jock armed with a Bren gun, he crawled along a shallow ditch at the foot of an embanked road. A machine-gunner, however, spotted and engaged Henderson, killing the Bren gunner and knocking Henderson's Webbly revolver out of his hand. The officer seizing his shovel from the back of his pack, charged the *Spandau*-gunner and sliced his head open with a blow from his shovel. Waving the patrol forward, he led them into a house at the edge of the village, before himself going back some sixty yards under heavy *Spandau* fire to recover the dead gunner's Bren gun. Lieutenant Henderson and his patrol were forced to abandon the building, which was on fire, as the *Fallschirmjäger* counter-attacked. They moved to another house, from which the enemy failed to move them. 'There it [the patrol] held out all day, and was finally caught up by the advance in the evening.' Lieutenant Henderson was awarded an immediate Distinguished Service Order for this determined action, which provides an insight into the nature and horror of close quarter battle.

By 0800 hours, with a very active and determined defence being mounted by the fanatical soldiers of *8th Fallschirmjäger Division*, 154 Brigade had a secure bridgehead but had failed to hold both Esserden and Speldrop. The loss of 1 Black Watch's artillery forward observation officer, without a doubt contributed to this, but immediate and ferocious counter-attacks were always to be expected from the Germans and the *Fallschirmjäger* in particular.

### 153 Brigade

Also crossing at 2100 hrs, Brigadier Roddie Sinclair was allocated the divisional main effort, the capture of the town of Rees and forming the easterly or right hand sector of the Highland Division's bridgehead. 5 Black Watch and 5/7 Gordon Highlanders, carried in 4 RTR's Buffaloes, were to land astride Rees. Crossing with the Brigade and under command, were the 3.7-inch howitzers of Captain McNair's 454 Mountain Battery RA. These were the only artillery guns that could be transported in the Buffaloes, as they could be dismantled and taken over obstacles, as generations of visitors to military tattoos knew (the Royal Navy gun team race is the only modern equivalent in

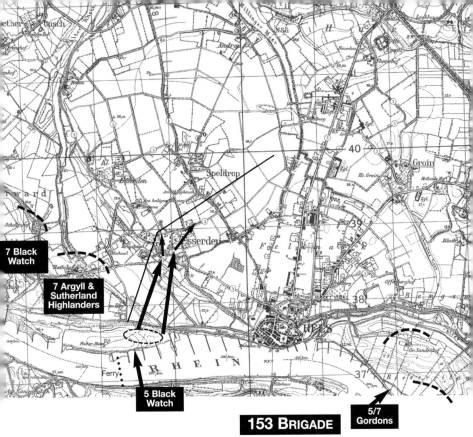

7 Black
Watch

7 Argyll &
Sutherland
Highlanders

5 Black
Watch

153 BRIGADE

5/7
Gordons

Ferry

current British Service). The role of the gunners, brought from training in the Inverness area, was to provide intimate support to 1 Gordons during the battle for Rees.

5 Black Watch had boarded their Buffaloes in some small woods south of the village of Appeldorn, three miles from the Rhine and had, as far as they were concerned, a good crossing. In fact 4 RTR had difficulty in climbing out of the river because of the stone clad enemy banks that damaged a high proportion of the LVT's tracks. This event of 'Clauswitzian friction' was to have a significant impact on subsequent operations. Debussing on the enemy bank, 5 Black Watch benefited from some very good reporting of likely enemy minefields by 3rd Division, that was based on observations of the areas where the Germans had been moving about without restriction. The Black Watch also benefited from the British barrage, which:

> ... had been murderously heavy; it had included salvos of rockets fired from tanks; much of the kick had been taken out of

79 ASLT SQN
GRAVESEND. M.R. E 059514

Esserden

To REES

D Coy
1 Gordons

5 Black
Watch

4 Royal Tank
Regt LVT

79 ASLT SQN
RE

GRAVESEND
FERRY SITE

HOME BANK

78

*the defence. The first companies passed over many positions whose garrisons were still dazed; as the succeeding companies reached them they were just coming to life.*

5 Black Watch's leading pair of companies set off towards their first objective a farm on the Esserden–Rees road. The remaining two companies who were following took over the lead towards the straggling village of Esserden. In close quarter battle they fought from building to building clearing out the *Fallschirmjäger* as they went. By dawn, they had cleared the southern half of the village of enemy. The regimental historian recorded: 'Here such few inhabitants as were left were weeping: they had been told by the parachutists that the British butchered all civilians. They went on weeping all night.' During the course of the early morning, 5 Black Watch forced the *Fallschirmjäger* out of the northern section of Esserden, completing their tasks.

Landing with 5 Black Watch were D Company 1 Gordons, who had accompanied them to secure a group of farm buildings which were to be used as a concentration area for the Gordons' attack on Rees from the west. They were to protect company recce groups and assault pioneers under Major Rae, who were to lift mines, lay out assembly lines and guide the companies forward as they landed. All did not, however, go to plan as the Germans set fire to the farm with incendiary bombs before D Company could secure the buildings, necessitating a change of position for the Forward Assembly Area (FAA) away from the blaze. Even so, D Company suffered casualties from mortar fire.

Carried across the Rhine by C Squadron 4 RTR, 5/7 Gordons landed on what was in effect an island to the east of Rees, bounded on its far side by a waterway, the Alter Rhine, which was the old course of the river. The battalion's objective was to clear the farmhouses on the island and hold the ground in order to isolate Rees from the east.

The Alter Rhine Island was held by a company of infantry, probably from 19 *Fallschirmjäger* Regiment, supplemented by *ersatz* infantry. The defences were centred around the farms of van Willichshof in the centre, Steppenhof in the south and Gross Sandenhof in the north, with section posts at key points along the bank.

The Gordons' regimental historian wrote:

*B Company, on the right, secured one farm within forty minutes of landing, a number of Germans being killed and forty*

**A young *Volkssturm (Hitlerjugend)* MG 34 crew.**

*taken. C Company made for the Alter Rhine to cross it and clear the further bank; but they found that the only bridge had been blown. As they approached they received heavy fire from the enemy beyond the stream. This was the first check. Meanwhile, D Company had arrived and taken another farm without opposition, and still another was captured, with fifteen Germans, by a platoon led by 2nd-Lieutenant Stephen.*

*When day broke on 24th March the Gordons were certainly in possession of the Island, but they spent an uneasy time upon it. From the higher ground beyond the Alter Rhine German*

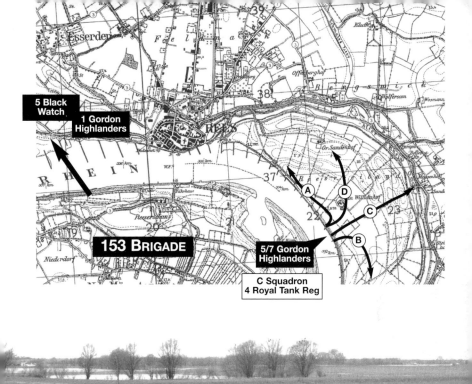

**5 Black Watch**

**1 Gordon Highlanders**

**153 Brigade**

**5/7 Gordon Highlanders**

**C Squadron 4 Royal Tank Reg**

A Ⓐ
D Ⓓ
C Ⓒ
B Ⓑ

**A view across the Alter Rhine Island showing how unpleasantly open it was for the 5/7 Gordons.**

*snipers and machine gunners commanded the whole expanse of open land: all movement outside the various farm buildings drew fire.*

Landing with the infantry of 153 Brigade were soldiers of the Royal Signals who had dragged an armoured telephone cable across the river, behind their Buffalo, to ensure line communications were maintained. Initially this was to be with the bank control officer and eventually with various headquarters that were to be established astride the Rhine.

### The Attack on Rees

The third battalion of 153 Brigade was 1 Gordons. They showered praise on '1 Royal Ulster Rifles, who held this sector of the near bank of the Rhine, for the Ulstermen not only dug slit trenches for the Gordons just behind the loading area but provided a special "brew up" so that every man received a mug of tea well laced with rum before embarking'. Major Martin Lindsay recalled that:

> I shall always remember the scene in the loading area: the massive bulk of the Buffaloes; the long ghostly files of men marching up to them, their flickering shadows and those of a smashed farmhouse and the armoured car at the Royals' post; a few busy figures darting here and there in the moonlight directing people into this and that Buffalo.

Then, as recorded by the regimental historian:

> ... came a delay. The first Buffaloes which returned from landing the Black Watch were not ready for the Gordons, for these craft found it difficult to get back out of the river on to the bank which was faced with stone. In attempting to land many of them damaged their tracks, and it was deemed quicker to bring along the Buffaloes which had already carried the 5th/7th Gordons across further up-stream. This check meant that the 1st Gordons could not start to attack Rees until 1 a.m. on 24th March and the respite must have been of value to the enemy.

Eventually, 1 Gordons successfully crossed the river without loss by 0050 hours and with a much delayed H Hour, B Company led the Battalion's advance towards the north west corner of Rees followed by C Company. Crossing three hundred yards of open grassland, the two companies were soon held up

**Looking due east towards Rees across the open ground that 1 Gordons had to cross.**

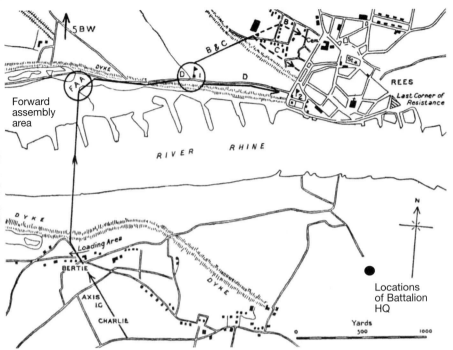

by enemy fire from the south west corner of Rees. However, under the cover of an on-call artillery bombardment and a mortar smoke screen, they crossed the open flood plain and cleared the winter dyke at 0153 hours, 'without further incident'. The winter bund was cleared with grenades and the Gordons pursued the enemy survivors who were falling back into their defensive perimeter in a housing estate.

At 0215 hours, B Company who were on the left flank, managed to get in amongst the houses and gardens of the estate under cover of darkness. Enemy resistance was very determined. They were in company strength and split up into groups of four to six, with each group occupying individual houses. Due to the dispersed nature of the estate, the enemy did not withdraw but stood and fought hard for each house they occupied and only surrendered when they were overrun. B Company itself only a hundred and twenty strong at the beginning of the battle took seventy *Fallschirmjäger* prisoner. It is not hard to work out who should have been labelled as 'elite' in this fight.

Meanwhile, at about 0400 hours, Major Lumsden's C Company had been able to follow a route parallel to the winter dyke south east into the centre of the town. They were, however, soon in trouble as their advance brought them under the fire of

**The area of the Cemetery (left) and the 'housing estate' (right) on the north western outskirts of Rees.**

snipers and machine guns not easy to locate on the outskirts of the ruin and chaos that was Rees. At 0445 hours, a platoon of C Company had broken into the western outskirts of Rees and was meeting stiff opposition. The enemy were 'using *Panzerfausts* at close range', in an anti-personnel role. Typically, as a section of Gordons entered a house they would be fired on by *Panzerfausts* from adjoining rooms, through 'mouseholes' in the walls. When they rallied and counter-attacked, they would find the defenders had escaped through prepared tunnels in the cellars.

By 0500 hours, both B and elements of C Companies were still spread out in the housing estate and the ground, north of the bund between the estate and the outskirts of the town. Opposition was still resolute and Major Lumsden had an additional problem. His rear platoon had been hit by a salvo of shells as they bunched up whilst crossing the bund. The platoon commander, Lieutenant Titterton, was dead and there were a dozen other casualties. The platoon had split up and dispersed either side of the bund.

Major Lindsay was monitoring the progress of the battle on the Battalion's radio net at Main HQ, which was still west of the river and recalled that:

> *The first intimation of trouble was Alec* [Lumsden] *asking*

*the Colonel to send up his spare officer, who had been left on the far bank with the company greatcoats and some other kit which they had taken across and dumped. Then he was telling D Company in the farmhouse area to send up part of one of his platoons, which had not crossed the dyke with the remainder. It was not hard to guess that this meant that the company had been shelled on its way forward, and that a platoon commander had been hit and some of the platoon had in consequence got lost or gone to ground. Meanwhile B and C Companies were fighting in the housing estate and gardens on the far side of the dyke and meeting a good deal of resistance. A little later ...it became apparent that C Company was still fighting in the orchards short of Rees when they came under fire from the Boche holding some of the houses at the outskirts of the town and by this time they were able to see well enough to shoot.*

Major Petrie, OC D Company, eventually gathered the remainder of C Company's last platoon and pushed up over the bund. When asked how things were going he admitted it was 'a bit sticky' but as it would be daylight shortly things might change. At first light, 0537 hours, however, the advantage switched decisively to the enemy who were now able to bring down accurate sniper and *spandau* fire on both B and C Companies. The penalty of the Gordons' delayed crossing was

**Fallschirmjäger** **artillery in action.**

now being paid!

At 0600 hours, C Company's position was being jeopardised by a group of Germans moving onto its left flank. B Company, who was still clearing the housing estate, had been unable to keep up with the C Company advance. Major Lindsay recalled:

> The next thing I heard was an acrimonious conversation between Alec Lumsden (C Company) and George Morrison (B). Alec was telling George that he hadn't put a platoon where he said he was going to, and that the enemy had in consequence been able to get round his flank [on the dyke]. He then spoke to the Colonel and said he was pinned down in the open with Huns on three sides of him and that he must withdraw on to B Company as he was getting casualties, could not get forward and his position was untenable. Having extracted a reluctant permission from the Colonel [Grant–Peterkin] to withdraw, he decided to hold on for a little longer, and then began to feel his way forward once more.

> About 5 a.m. I heard him [Lumsden] report that he had reached the first row of houses in the town. Later on I heard B Company say they had passed through the cemetery and reached the edge of Rees, having taken about seventy prisoners. An hour or two after that Bowlby said he gathered that D Company had also reached the town, along the water's edge.

It was at about this time that Major Morrison, was bursting into a house through the front door, '... when I was bowled over by a German who was coming out. He was a giant of a man, a *Fallschirmjäger* sergeant major, carrying a *Schmeisser* sub machine gun'. To everyone's surprise, it was the wiry Scottish major who got up from the ensuing brief but brutal struggle. Soon afterwards, the resistance in the housing estate crumbled and the left flank of C Company was able to break into the edge of the town.

**The face of a *Fallschirmjäger* soldier fighting the Fatherland's invaders.**

B Company reported at 0700 hours, that they had reached the Rees-Speldrop road and turning right, had positioned themselves in the Rees cemetery and were deployed to protect the flank of C Company who were to fight their way into the main part of the town. German resistance was, however, far from crushed and the capture of Rees was going to be a protracted affair.

**Strongly built houses on the edge of town made good strongpoints for the enemy.**

### DD Tanks

Meanwhile, the two squadrons of DD tanks belonging to Lieutenant-Colonel John Trotter's Staffordshire Yeomanry, had started the process of crossing the river behind and between the two infantry brigades. Their entry point was near what was referred to as 'Storm Boat House'. Troop Commander, Lieutenant Sadler, described the operation:

> *We sent a recce party over with the Buffaloes, to pick landing spots which were supposed to be lit with green lights, two green lights, one above the other.*

The Staffordshire Yeomanry were responsible for making their own exits and the recce and preparatory work on the banks, the far bank took a considerable amount of time and in many cases, unaided, the tanks found the exit bank to be difficult. However, crossing in one of the Yeomanry's six Buffaloes was an airborne bulldozer, which was light enough to cross the mud banks. Once ashore, it was able to reduce the bank to a slope and several carpets made of coir matting with scaffolding poles were laid to give rigidity. With the exits made, the tanks could cross. Lieutenant Sadler continued:

> *I was first tank into the River. We went down the slope, on the way we had quite a bit of gunfire and one or two of the tanks had their canvas screens holed so they couldn't do the trip.*
>
> *We got into the river, which was quite fast flowing. I seemed to have been there a long time and I didn't see the two green lights, but suddenly I saw one green light. I thought, well, the other one might have gone out or something, so I started to land*

*and I found out I was on a mud bank. Before I realised where I was (I thought I'd crossed the river), I let the canvas side down and of course my other two tanks, or three in actual fact, came over and one got stuck in the mud. There was a shellfire going on at that time. It was very uncomfortable and I had to get out of the tank, get the chains out and hook on to the other tank and pull it out. Of course, then I had the problem of whether to risk going from the mud bank to the actual true bank of the river. I probably didn't have enough air anyway to inflate the screen again, so I took the chance and as it happened, the water didn't come up above turret level so we were all right. The other three tanks followed.*

*The actual place I landed, of course, was wrong. The correct place was about two hundred yards downstream. I went down and was able to link up with them, by which time, the squadron leader had arrived.*

The difficulty in locating the DD exit point was due to the fact that it was not directly or even obliquely across the river but almost a mile downstream. The 3 $\frac{1}{2}$ knot current swept the ungainly and barely 'seaworthy' tanks downstream through the 154 Brigade LVT crossing loop.

When the first tank was eventually ashore, at the correct point, it was used to help tow other DDs across the soft river mud and onto the ramp over the Rhine dyke. By 0600 hours, two troops of the Staffordshire Yeomanry's DD tanks were across and ready for action. With the laying of the coir carpets further out into the river and with daylight, the speed of crossing increased markedly and the first squadron was supporting the infantry at 0700 hours. The DD converted Shermans, despite the problems on the exit banks and the loss of

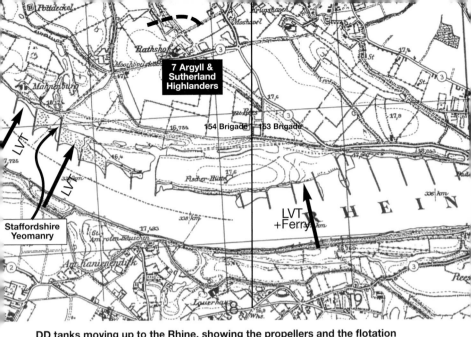

7 Argyll & Sutherland Highlanders

154 Brigade — 153 Brigade

LVT

LVT

Staffordshire Yeomanry

LVT +Ferry

R H E I N

DD tanks moving up to the Rhine, showing the propellers and the flotation screen in the lowered position.

**Staffordshire Yeomanry DD crews deflating their flotation screens following their crossing.**

three tanks, had been used to help solve the perennial problem of assault crossings of major waterways; being able to get tanks across in time for them to be available to help defeat enemy counter-attacks. The remaining two squadrons would not be able to cross until 13 Army Group Royal Engineers opened their Class 50/60 ferries which would not be before H Hour +12.

### 152 Brigade

Brigadier Cassels did, however, have an active role in the initial stages of the assault. He was, however, to provide a battalion (2 Seaforth) under command of 153 Brigade, to assist in the isolation of Rees and 5 Cameronian to 154 Brigade to further expand the bridgehead. With his remaining battalion (5 Seaforth), he was to maintain a divisional reserve and be prepared to lead the development of operations from the divisional bridgehead.

As the fourth battalions of the two assault brigades, the Seaforths and the Cameronians crossed the river in a ferry of storm boats operated by 70 Field Company RE. The ferry site was approximately on the inter-brigade boundary, which aided command and control in the dark. 'Thirty-five boats and engines had been brought forward during the night before the assault, under cover of smoke, and dumped and camouflaged in the orchard behind the proposed launching site near Storm Boat House.' According to the RE history:

> About an hour after the assault waves of Buffaloes had crossed, the boats were carried over the dyke with the help of a company of pioneers and, by 2315 hours, twenty-two serviceable boats were in the water.
>
> All boats were concentrated to run a continuous ferry service. Bank Control allotted the ferry to one battalion at a time, with the leading battalion of 152 Brigade moving up and commencing to cross at 0035 hours 24 March.

Highland troops were marshalled into boats as they became available and the loaded boats crossed one behind the other to the landing places on the far bank, 'which had been marked upstream and downstream by carefully shaded coloured lights'. Only the most important light vehicles were ferried across in LVTs at this stage, which left the infantry battalions to man-pack their machine guns and mortars, along with their ammunition. With only light scales of ammunition, their own organic fire support was limited.

> The boats continued to operate backwards and forwards. It was found that it took about 55 minutes to ferry a battalion across the river and, with some breaks in operating, the six battalions of 152 Brigade and 9 Canadian Brigade as well as some 500 other troops had been ferried across by the afternoon of 24 March. Prisoners and casualties were brought back on return journeys.

The ferrying operation was 'peaceful while the first battalion was being taken over but the site was a very obvious one and soon became subjected to very accurate shelling which continued, off and on, well into 24 March'.

Captain Stafford, who was the far bank recce party for a heavy class 50 (tons) ferry, codenamed TILBURY, that was to be operated in the area of 152 Brigades assault the following day could testify that things did not remain 'peaceful' for long.

> On touching down on the enemy bank, we immediately found that the initial wave of infantry had encountered a schumine field on the beach, and several men had been killed or wounded in it. ... Owing to the minefields, I decided that our quickest and safest method of progress was to wade in the river, where it was unlikely that we would encounter any enemy obstructions. We

**Medium and heavy ferries would not be open for many hours, making the DD tanks an important asset.**

*soon found this easier said than done, mainly due to the weight and clumsiness of the equipment we were carrying. Mortar fire was becoming increasingly accurate and more than once I had to perform the divers act to protect myself. In doing this, I lost my 38 [radio] Set which had been strapped on my back. Every 150 yards or so, we encountered groins and, as we crossed the first one, I became aware that something was disclosing our exact position, as a sniper, hiding in a nearby crane, appeared to have our range very accurately. On investigation, I discovered the reason – every time I stooped down, a hand torch on the rear of my belt switched on, flashing out a vivid green light! Even so, we were increasingly troubled by accurate mortar fire.*

While 2 Seaforth were across the river quickly around the appointed hour of 0235 hours, 5 Camerons prepared to cross around 0300 hours and HQ 152 Brigade and 5 Seaforth (divisional reserve) not until dawn. This last battalion went across in dribs and drabs due to the losses to storm boats and the fifty casualties amongst the Sappers of 70 Field Company, which reduced the number ferrying to twelve. The Seaforth's historian recorded that:

> The Battalion crossed company by company and disembarked on the far bank under intermittent shell fire, a few casualties being suffered. As soon as the stragglers, from a wayward boat, had been collected, the Battalion moved up the axis of 5th Black Watch, to a forming-up area in Esserden. We had sent a party, under the Second-in-Command, with the rear elements of 5th Black Watch to reconnoitre and prepare a forming-up place, within the perimeter of 5th Black Watch's area. C Company, our reinforcement Company, had been employed launching the boats, after which they provided guides for the assaulting waves down to the riverside.

See map on page 95

At 0245 hours, A Company 2 Seaforth set out to seal off the northern approaches to Rees via an unnamed crossroads that was nicknamed 'Bill' and a bridge over the anti-tank ditch, which was in fact an existing water course that had been improved for defence. Here A Company contacted small parties of *Fallschirmjäger* who were promptly dealt with. The Seaforth were, however, in an unenviably precarious position.

> It was not thought that the mopping-up of Rees, by the remaining Battalions of 153 Brigade, would be completed by the time the Battalion set out on its mission, and we were prepared for an unprotected right flank on our move. It had been planned, however, that a Battalion of 154 Brigade on the left [1 Black Watch] would be holding Speldrop, by the time we were launched, thus protecting our left flank. As it turned out,

*Speldrop did not fall until nearly 36 hours later and we went into our task with two open flanks.*

*We were of course operating in the dark and were equipped and prepared to force our way to our objective, there to remain in hedgehog fashion, astride the main road, until the Battalions, fighting in Rees, could fight their way through to us, or we to them.*

Battalion Headquarters and the remaining two Companies, D and B, were poised ready to pass through B Company and continue quickly to their objective, the factory north of Rees. The bridge over the anti-tank ditch was, however, found to be badly blown and the road cratered. This did not delay the infantry companies, although it meant a good deal of engineer work, before the battalion HQ vehicles could pass. Under fire, a platoon of sappers, under command, started work immediately. A Sapper officer was 'having an exciting chase with a sniper, rounded off by measuring his length in the water at the bottom of the ditch'.

By dawn 2 Seaforth had moved a mile inland and were astride the old B67 (east of the modern road of that designation) and had overcome stiff resistance in the Pipe Factory.

*D Company reached the main road and B Company their objective, the latter going through to capture intact the road bridge, over the [another] anti-tank ditch, North of the position.*

**The 'anti-tank ditch' is today back in use as a drainage ditch.**

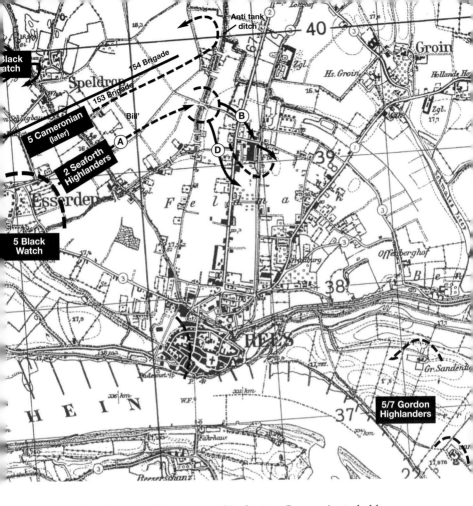

The objective was a big one – too big for two Companies to hold, so the Commanding Officer, Lieutenant Colonel GW Dunn, ordered up A Company (less a Platoon which remained to protect our axis) to another area east of the Factory. The Battalion thus disposed had only just consolidated when dawn broke. The enemy was clearly thrown out of gear by the arrival of the Battalion across their main line of retreat, and some 50-60 prisoners were taken within a short time, most of them walking blindly into the trap set for them. At dawn, it was seen that quite a large number of enemy were all round us, and our axis of advance, the previous night, was under constant small arms fire. Further, the two Battalions clearing Rees had their hands full in the town and seemed unlikely to reach us that day.

95

A *Fallschirmjäger* medium mortar crew preparing their ammunition.

Lieutenant Colonel Dunn's aggressive tactics and local patrols cleared the whole of the Pipe Factory complex and the immediate surrounding area. This was a commendable result as it was a big task, and further prisoners were rounded up. The Seaforths requested a troop of tanks in order to extend their domination of the surrounding country but, none were yet

Crossroads "Bill"        Factories        Rees

A Coy
2 Seaforth
Highlanders

available, so the battalion 'had just to sit in their hedgehog' defences, without transport of any description with them. To keep the enemy quiet, and take what local offensive action they could, patrols probed outwards. The enemy engaged the Seaforths with *Spandau* fire and casualties were suffered who could not be evacuated, leaving the Regimental Medical Officer with a growing number of men to treat with his scant man-packed resources.

To the east a significant number of enemy troops were seen moving on the Groin road running north out of Rees throughout the day. Signal communication was reasonably good because both Seaforth's Tactical HQ and the attached gunner observation party had carried the heavy sets forward from the blown bridge, either on man-packs, or on improvised trolleys. Using the radios, the withdrawing Germans were engaged by observed artillery fire.

By placing themselves across the B67, 2 Seaforth had started the isolation of Rees from the north, leaving a one mile gap to the north-east between them and 5/7 Gordons on the Island. A gap that was covered by fire from machine guns and artillery. 2 Seaforth, however, were isolated but it was expected that their situation would improve when 5 Cameronian seized the hamlet of Mittelburg to the north, which once in a state of defence, would offer a degree of mutual support.

5 Cameronian moving up behind 5 Black Watch in Esserden found that fighting was still going on in the area and that it was not possible to advance on Mittelburg as planned at first light (0530 hrs). However, the Staffordshire Yeomanry's DD tanks were now arriving in the bridgehead and the first squadron was duly allocated to the Cameronians for their delayed attack which was now due to start at 0700 hours.

With the tanks moving by bounds, supporting the infantry, the 5 Cameronian battle group advanced on the village of Mittelburg. As they approached, four or five assault guns opened fire from positions amongst the houses at the edge of the village. These assault guns were almost certainly from *15 Panzer Grenadier Division*. The battle group possessing superior firepower, in the form of the Shermans of B Squadron and, of course, the corps artillery, was able to continue the advance. However, on closing up to the anti-tank ditch three out of four Yeomanry tanks were knocked out and the attack over the open ground came to a halt. It is probable that the assault guns were either the self-same vehicles or were from the company that supported the counter-attack on Speldrop and Klein Esserden just a little later. With the situation at Speldrop to their left rear deteriorating and *Spandaus* sweeping the open terrain they would have to cover to reach Mittelburg, the decision was made to abandon further advances by 5 Cameronian. This of course left 2 Seaforth isolated in the Pipe Factory in what their CO described as a 'sticky position'.

At about 0800 hours the Seaforth and Cameronians reverted to command of 152 Brigade, once Tactical Headquarters and 5 Seaforth had crossed the river after dawn, in penny packets due to the loss of so many storm boats.

### 9 Canadian Brigade

Meanwhile, the highland battalions of 9 Canadian Brigade, 3rd Canadian Division were crossing the Rhine behind 154 Brigade on the left flank of the assault. The Highland Light Infantry of Canada's (HLI of C) advance party, consisting of nine other ranks commanded by Capt Donald Pearce, had gone ahead with elements of 154 Bde and were waiting on the east bank. Their task was to recce the ground in order to lead the battalion to its assembly area when it arrived on the far side. These men were the first Canadians to cross the Rhine.

At 0345 hours, the HLI of C received orders to move, and by

**The prime means of movement for both sides was marching.**

0425 hours the fighting men of the four rifle companies with 'Mae West' lifejackets slung round them and laden with 24-hour ration packs, were clambering into their Buffaloes in the marshalling area on the road north of Honnopel. Having driven four hundred yards over the flood plain they had crossed the Rhine under 'sporadic shelling'. An hour later, once on the far bank, guides led the battalion into its assembly area to the south of Klein Esserden, a march that was enlivened for C Company capturing of 30 members of the *Volkssturm*. Here, fully assembled as dawn broke, the Highland Light Infantry of Canada came under command of 154 Brigade, at a crucial point in the battle; reports were coming in of 1 Black Watch's difficulties at Speldrop. The original tasks allocated to the battalion in the expansion of the bridgehead, the capture of Bienen were now impractical and the battalion monitored the situation. Eventually, as we will see in Chapter 9, warning orders were issued and plans made to retake Speldrop.

The remainder of 9 Canadian Brigade were scheduled to cross later in the day and to be complete by mid afternoon.

## Summary

Enemy reaction to the 51st Highland Division's crossing in the Rees sector had at first been slight, due to a combination of the numbing effect of the bombardment, tactical surprise and the isolation of the battlefield, the interdiction sorties flown by the Allied air forces. However, the German response by local reserves was increasingly significant and supported with mortar fire and by sniping from determined *Fallschirmjäger* soldiers. There were also signs that the inevitable armoured counter-attacks were developing.

By 0800 hours, however, 51st Highland Division had secured a bridgehead with the majority of its infantry, with mainly man-packable support weapons. However, they were well served by a mass of artillery whose radio nets in most cases were working well and some tank support. Other heavy weapons and vehicles, along with the ordinary gun tanks of the Northamptonshire Yeomanry would have to await the opening of ferries before they could cross to the east bank of the river. The nature of the country, with its boggy terrain and defended villages and woods, was such that the two squadrons of DD tanks were very much in a supporting role in case of counter-

**Officers of the Highland Light Infantry of Canada.**

attack. The leading elements of 9 Canadian Brigade were also across and with 152 Brigade now operational, sufficient combat power was being assembled to hold anything *15th Panzergrenadiers* and *8th Fallschirmjäger* could throw at the Highland Division. Meanwhile, 1 Gordons were in the first phase of clearing the virtually isolated town of Rees, which it was now acknowledged would be a slow business.

### The Death of General Rennie

The 51st Highland Division had been subject to numerous changes of command. Major General Thomas Rennie was moved from 3rd Division and is widely credited with restoring the fame and fortune of the Division.

He was often to be found at the sharp end, encouraging his Jocks across the start line and visiting front line positions, leaving the infantry knowing that he shared their dangers and hardships.

At 0900 hours on the morning of 24 March, General Rennie had crossed the Rhine with his Jeep in an LVT and was on his way to visit Tac HQ of 154 Brigade. In the jeep along with the General were Lieutenant Tweedie, his ADC, and his radio operator, Lance-Corporal Craig. Still in the area of the riverbank, he wished 'Good luck' to the Adjutant of 7 Argylls, who was passing in a Bren gun carrier and as the divisional historian recalled:

> A salvo of mortar bombs fell, and the jeep received a direct hit. General Rennie fell out on to the grass verge. Tweedie was unhurt, but Craig was wounded. "Are you all right, sir?" asked Tweedie. There was no reply. General Rennie was carried to 176 Field Ambulance, which was only some thirty yards away. He died almost immediately after admission.

General Horrocks wrote 'I have always felt that Rennie had some foreboding about this battle ... I had never seen him so worried. He hated everything about it and I couldn't understand why. Like so many highlanders I believe he was "Fey".'

The shocking loss of such a fearless, popular and effective divisional commander can be imagined. For instance, Colonel Bradford of 5 Black Watch, told his company commanders of the General's death 'but forbade them to pass it on to the Jocks until

Rees should be taken'. Perhaps this passage will explain Colonel Bradford's fears:

> There was never anybody quite like Thomas Rennie. He was as staunch as Dumbarton Rock, determined to the point of obstinacy; he was a great Jock-lover, and they in turn adored him. He was the most accessible and least pretentious of generals, of whom every officer and man could boast as a friend. He had an impish sense of humour, and a cheerfulness, which was proof against every crisis or disaster. He had a great flair for doing things the right way, and complete confidence in his judgment, which was shared by all around him. He could sift the essential from the non-essential, and refused to bother himself at all or take the slightest interest in anything which was not. His courage was far beyond the ordinary, but there was nothing flamboyant about him. ... there wasn't a Jock in the Division who did not know his duffle-coated figure. He never wore a red hat to the day of his death; a Red Hackle was good enough for him.

General Rennie was buried at the village of Appeldorn on the west bank, with four Black Watch soldiers acting as pallbearers, to the sound of the pipes. Attending were his divisional staff, General Horrocks, his Corps Commander, and the commanders of the 3rd British Division and 3rd Canadian Division. During the post war concentration of graves, his body was moved to the CWGC cemetery in the Reichswald.

# Chapter 5

# Operation WIDGEON

UNDER THE COMMAND of 12 Corps, 1 Commando Brigade was to conduct another important preliminary assault crossing of the Rhine an hour after the initial assault by 51st Highland Division and ten miles up stream. Brigadier Mills-Roberts was given the task of seizing the town of Wesel, an important communications centre on the east bank, which was a strongpoint that, if not captured promptly, would dominate important crossing and bridging points and routes in the centre of 21st Army Group's area of operations.

Lieutenant General Ritchie, Commander XII Corps:

> ... had given it as his considered opinion that the whole of the operation as it affected his formation depended on this assault being successful. It was considered too, that the success of the attack on the town depended in turn largely on the success of two very heavy bombing raids on the area.

**Brigadier Mills-Roberts.**

At Wesel the Rhine was a little narrower than elsewhere, at about two hundred yards wide but the speed through the narrower channel was slightly higher at around five knots. As usual the river was prevented from flooding the surrounding country by dykes, from fifteen to twenty feet in height. While the town was built on the banks of the river behind high dykes, to the north west, there were in the surrounding area the usual several hundred yards of open flood plains. Wesel itself was a medium size town of some twenty-four thousand inhabitants. The old town, much of it medieval, was strongly built, largely of stone, but with a high

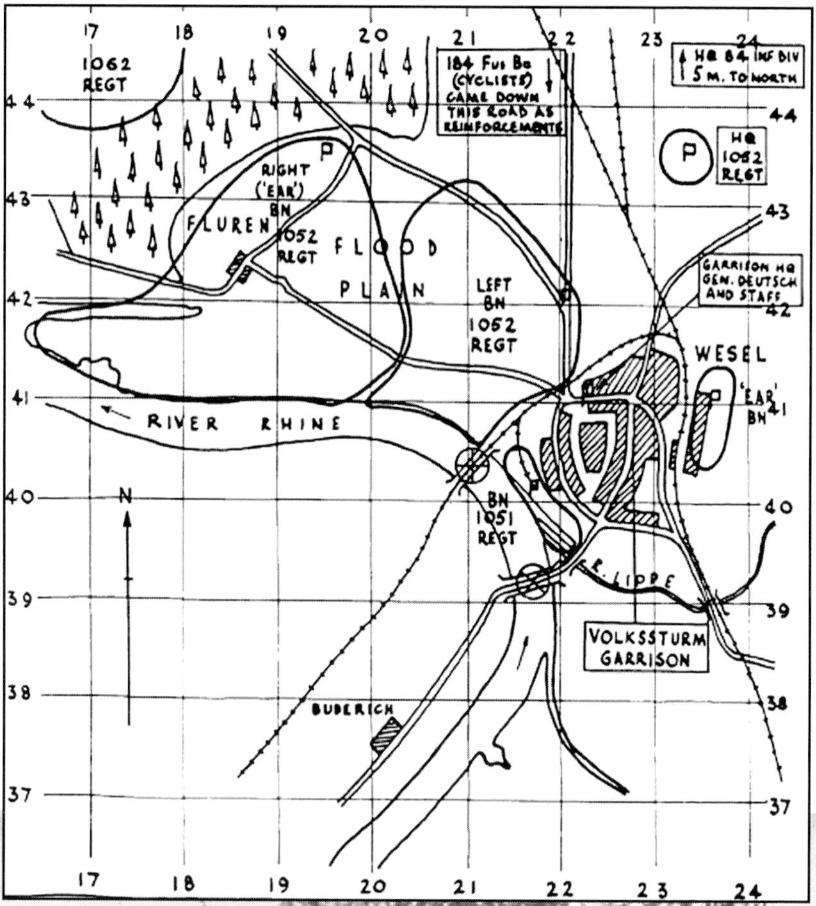
1062 REGT
184 Fus Bn (CYCLISTS) CAME DOWN THIS ROAD AS REINFORCEMENTS
HQ 84 INF DIV 5 M. TO NORTH
HQ 1052 REGT
RIGHT ('EAR') BN 1052 REGT
FLUREN
FLOOD PLAIN
LEFT BN 1052 REGT
GARRISON HQ GEN. DEUTSCH AND STAFF
WESEL
'EAR' BN
RIVER RHINE
N
BN 1051 REGT
R. LIPPE
VOLKSSTURM GARRISON
BUDERICH

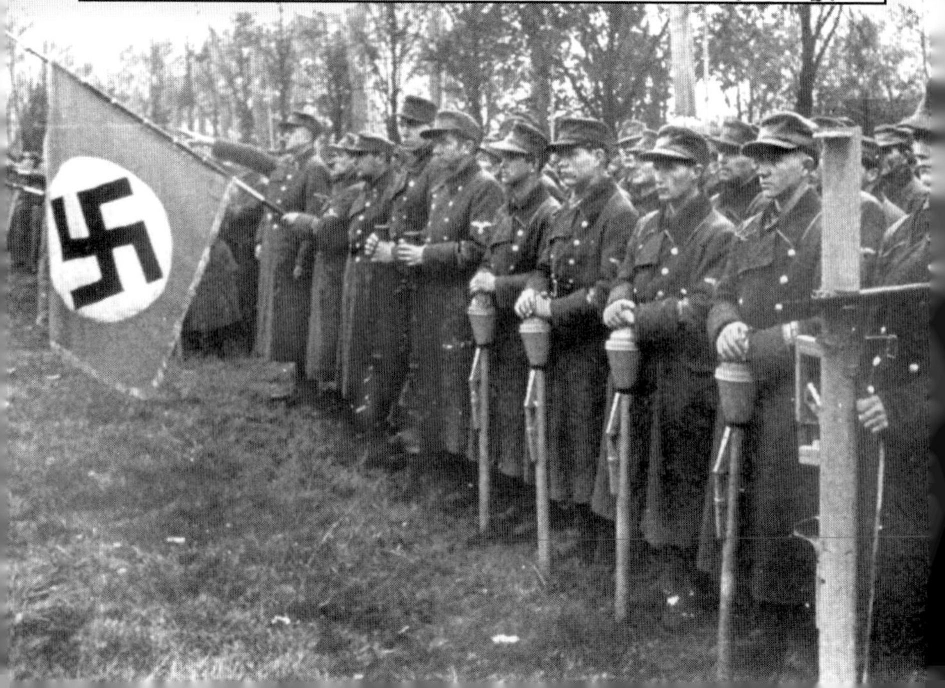

proportion of wood. Like most towns on the Rhine, Wesel had already received the attentions of the Allied air forces, finally by 77 Lancasters of No. 3 Group on the afternoon immediately before the attack.

There was not much information on the dispositions of the enemy in the town, which was in the sector thought to be held by Major-General Heinz Fiebig's *84th Volksgrenadier Division*. In fact the town had its own garrison of *volkssturm*, under Major General Deutch, with at least one of the numerous *ersatz* battalions (probably 317th), made up of administrative troops extracted from the rear areas. Brigadier Mills-Roberts wrote:

> When I was eventually told to make my preliminary recce I walked through the small riverside villages, which nestled beneath the enormous flood dyke on our side of the river... . Looking across the river, I saw the town of Wesel, with the tall spires of several churches. It was going to be difficult to marshal our 1,600 men for the crossing without being observed by the Germans.

Using air photographs and maps he and his commanding officers,

> ... could barely see the enemy defences at this distance but with the help of our marked maps we could see that the flood plain was defended by a trench system close to the river bank itself, while further back were two large isolated waterman's houses garrisoned by stronger forces. There were even stronger German forces further back, where the flood plain merged with higher ground. And I could see that a frontal assault on the town of Wesel was virtually impossible – the Germans had taken elaborate precautions against such an emergency.

### 1 Commando Brigade's Plan

The mission given to 1 Commando Brigade was 'to seize Wesel and hold the eastern and southern exits of the town'. Brigadier Mills-Roberts' recce and appreciation led him to base his brigade plan on five points: first, that to take full advantage of the bombing raids the Commando brigade was to cross the river before the second raid and form up ready to rush into the city while its defences were still 'punch drunk'; secondly, to achieve surprise, it was decided to cross at the most unlikely spot, some open and

**1 Commando Brigade shoulder flash.**

muddy flood plain two miles west of Wesel; thirdly, there was to be no attempt to secure the entire town, as it would not be possible to clear the whole area, before the inevitable counter-attacks; the brigade would therefore seize a compact area including a large factory area dominating the northern approaches to Wesel; fourthly, there should be no trace of the Brigade on the flood plain at dawn, leaving the Germans unaware of their strength and whereabouts. This meant that the commandos would have to carry their own supplies, as a ferry would not be established until the town was clear. Fifthly, Mills-Roberts knew that by landing across the muddy flood plain he would be unable to take heavy weapons on the crossing. He believed, however, that the German armour would have been drawn away by 51st Highland Division's landing and that they would wish to avoid the risk of fighting in the rubble of an urban area where they would be vulnerable. Consequently, with limited carrying capacity and the river mud, the anti-tank guns were to be left behind but it was, however, expected that the ubiquitous German *Panzerfausts* would be captured in large numbers from the defenders, which could be used by the commandos in extremis.

The four commando units, 45 and 46 Commandos Royal Marines and Nos. 3 and 6 (Army) Commandos, were joined by, amongst others, 84 Field Company RE and parties from a Mountain Regiment RA. This regiment, the nearest thing to commando gunners at that time, would provide forward observation parties and direct fire support. Their rear link from Brigade HQ, to Regimental HQ and CRA 12 Corps, on whom the commandos relied for their heavy fire support was vital. The LVTs allocated to the Brigade were to be operated by 77 Assault Squadron RE, who had sufficient vehicles to carry a single commando across the river in one lift before returning to collect the next of two waves.

Brigadier Mills-Roberts summarised his plan:

*I decided to send 46 Commando over first in the Buffaloes and go with them with a small Brigade Headquarters. No. 46 had to capture the bank of the river and 6 Commando – which would be next ashore from the storm boats – had to sweep up the river bank and enter Wesel. The other two commandos would be brought across the river by the Buffalo ferry.*

Having captured much of the town, re-enforcement of the lightly armed commandos, was to come in the form of 1 Cheshires being ferried across the river at the earliest opportunity. Meanwhile, 17th US Airborne Division was to drop north of Wesel at 1000 hours and link up with the Commando Brigade in the northern part of the town. The airborne drop would take between three and four hours, during which artillery fire would not be possible. For that period, the Commando Brigade would have to hold on to Wesel without fire support.

**Commando qualification badge.**

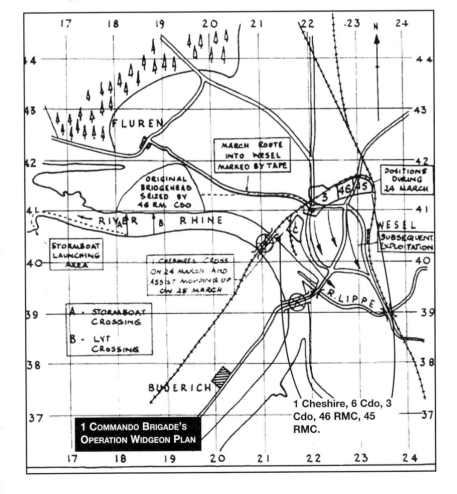

**1 COMMANDO BRIGADE'S OPERATION WIDGEON PLAN**

1 Cheshire, 6 Cdo, 3 Cdo, 46 RMC, 45 RMC.

Looking back across the Rhine to the Home Bank and the dyke walls.

LVTs preparing for the Rhine crossing.

The view across the Rhine from Grau Insel.

## The Crossing

With the codeword confirming that the operation was on, finally being received at 1715 hours, the battle was started at 1730 hours by the afternoon air raid on Wesel by medium bombers. Mills-Roberts commented that 'It was a short sharp attack, lasting fifteen minutes'. The Commandos watched from their hide locations, the procession of a hundred aircraft going over to their target in a steady stream. As the drone of aero engines faded 'a great pall of dust hung over the city'. At 1800 hours, the artillery bombardment started and 'from that moment the roll of gun fire until long after H-hour was continuous'.

Bill Sadler of No. 6 Commando recalled the march from their Assembly Area down to the Rhine:

*After some miles of continuous marching, the packs and equipment began to assume twice their original proportions and weight but shortly before reaching the river, a halt was called to supply the column with some unexpected and welcome refreshment. Our packs and equipment were left in position to move off again, while each man collected his issue of tea, rum (a dessertspoon of rum – a life-giving fluid) and sandwiches – the last bread we would see until the end of the war.*

There is some evidence that a mere dessertspoonful of rum, as issued to the commandos, was meagre, when compared with that issued elsewhere to the assault troops.

The loads carried by the Commandos were considerable. For instance, No. 5 (Heavy Weapons) Troop of 6 Commando, manhandled two medium machine guns, along with their tripods, sights, ammunition and three 'K-guns', with an ample supply of preloaded reserve magazines, so that each man in the troop was carrying at least 100 pounds.

Meanwhile, Brigadier Mills-Roberts with his tactical HQ, along with Major Ted Rushton of 3rd Mountain Regiment and his signals detachment, embarked in the Buffaloes carrying 46 Commando RM. Time dragged around to H Hour. Mills-Roberts recalled the final wait and the move to the river:

> I looked at my watch – ten minutes to go – we were due off at 2200 hours. I said to Donald, "My watch has stopped." We checked. "No" he said. "This is a long ten minutes."
>
> The Buffaloes were now warming up ... the large vehicles lurched forward. Our driver put his foot down and soon in front of us loomed the dyke. The momentum we carried sent us three quarters of the way and then we slid drunkenly back to the bottom, but the driver took another run and this time there was no mistake.

All accounts of the crossing describe how the 25-pounder shells of 6 Field Regiment, who were firing at a rapid rate for ten minutes, were bursting on the bank opposite and drowning out the sound of everything else. Suddenly the area was lit up by fifteen foot flames from a direct hit from an enemy mortar on one of the Buffaloes ahead on the far river bank. This beacon-like blaze attracted the Germans' attention and brought further shells and mortar bombs.

Captain Gibbon, an Army commando attached from the Border Regiment, commanding B Troop, was the first man of 46 Commando to leap ashore. The Germans in the trenches on the river bank were stunned by the bombardment and within a few minutes, Captain Pierce RM, at the head of Y Troop, had rounded up sixty-five prisoners. Meanwhile, Captain Gibbon was pushing inland with B Troop. His artillery forward observation officer and his signallers had been in the Buffalo which had been hit, and he was, consequently, unable to call for fire support. Realising this, he led his men close under the pre-planned creeping barrage and reached the assault position for their objective, the Wardmann's Haus, five hundred yards from the river bank, while shells were still bursting around it. So close

**Wardmann's Haus just inland from 46 Commando's landing point.**

to their own fire was B Troop that their sergeant major and
another man from Troop HQ were killed approaching the
building. The fighting around the first Wardmann's Haus was
over quickly, with the defenders, a company HQ and two
platoons, being overwhelmed by the Commando's aggression.
The last of them surrendered promptly when their commander
was killed and grenades were thrown into the cellar. Some sixty
Germans were taken prisoner, including two officers.

Meanwhile, the second flight of Buffaloes, carrying the rest of
46 Commando, had by now landed. A and Z Troops moved
across the flood plain to their objective, the second Wardmann's
Haus about a thousand yards from the landing point. It was
quickly secured and the A Troop swung left and overran a light
flak position that had been causing trouble. Z Troop passed
through to consolidate their sector of the perimeter. By 2215
hours, 46 Commando RM had established a bridgehead, into

which the remainder of the Brigade would land and assemble for the next phase of the operation. Brigadier Mills-Roberts said 'We had been ashore for less than a quarter of an hour, but we had no time to lose'.

The other brigade units crossed as planned. No. 6 Commando was allocated storm boats, while No. 45 Commando RM had had the convenience of the Buffaloes. The storm boats were launched in a lagoon some two thousand yards downstream of the crossing place. The boats were to move down the lagoon at full speed, up stream, stop, pick up No. 6 Commando, and then cross the Rhine. The Commanding Officer Lieutenant Colonel Lewis recalls that excessive speed led to an unfortunate incident:

> One boat was overloaded. When the driver took off, the thing drove straight under water. Many of the men had their bregans still on their backs (instead of loosening them as they were meant to once they got aboard), and some were drowned with the weight of them.

Out in the main river, the boats were seen almost at once by the enemy, who opened fire. In addition, some storm boats were hit by smallarms fire, and one sank with its motor still running, drowning Lieutenant Hume-Spry and several of his section. RSM Woodcock had three boats shot under him before he landed on the enemy bank.

The difficulties of the crossing were, as predicted, increased by the breakdown of many of the outboard motors. Following similar experiences of mechanical breakdown during training, despite stripping down and thorough servicing, the outboard engines proved to be unreliable as expected. Small Dory craft, used by the commandos in coastal raids, had been brought to the Rhine for use as rescue boats, were soon proving their worth and vindicating Brigadier Mills-Roberts, who had insisted on them. Most of No. 6 Commando, was, however, across the river in fifteen minutes.

Meanwhile, having dropped off 45 Commando, the Buffaloes of 77 Assault Squadron, returned to the home bank and ferried across the final unit of the Brigade, No. 3 Commando. The ferrying operation, which was crucial to the Commando Brigade's clearance of the open approaches and establishing themselves in the town, was carried out in an exemplary manner.

BBC correspondent Stewart MacPherson was watching the crossing from the home bank and recorded the following:

*I watched the [last] commandos take off for Wesel ... . A few minutes after they were due to arrive on the far side, bomber command were to deliver a crushing blow on the enemy in Wesel, while the commandos lay doggo over there, a bare thousand yards from the bomber target, and waited. Smack on time, Arthur Harris & Company, House Removers, as they were called by the commandos, arrived and delivered a nerve-shaking blow on the former Wesel stronghold. Back at Headquarters, minutes ticked by. Officers waited anxiously for word from the commandos across the river. Suddenly there was a signal, and a voice literally purred over the wireless: 'Noisy blighters, aren't they?'*

The 'noisy blighters', 201 RAF heavy bombers, arrived at 2230 hours and dropped 1,100 tons of bombs. The Army had in fact requested a raid of only 300 tons of high explosive. Mills-Roberts described the attack in slightly more technical terms:

*We saw the Pathfinder aircraft of Bomber Command drop their red flare markers over the town. These were followed a few seconds later by two hundred Lancasters, each with a double block-buster load. As the bombs dropped, showers of debris flew into the air accompanied by great banks of fire. The noise was colossal and the ground shook under us although we were a thousand yards away – which was the margin allowed by Bomber Command. The whole plain was illuminated by a red, lurid glow.*

'It seemed,' said Major Bartholomew, 'as if more than mortal powers had been unleashed.'

While the heavy bombing of the town was in progress, the commandos had waited on the 'safety line', with the nearest troops only 1,250 yards away from the aiming point. This precision raid by RAF Bomber Command was the closest ever made to ground troops and quite remarkable when it is recalled that in 1942, the RAF classed as a hit, any bombs on a night raid that landed within five miles of its target!

The devastation of Wesel was almost complete but the rubble provided cover for the enemy.

A member of the *Volkssturm* armed with a *panzerfaust*.

As the last bombers approached Wesel at 2230 hours, No. 6 Commando was poised to move forward toward the town. The atmosphere was still laden with dust and smoke, as No. 6 Commando set off, with a sub section of 6 Troop under Lance Sergeant Tonse leading the way, as the bombers were completing their final run. Their Commanding Officer, Lieutenant Colonel Lewis of the Dorset Regiment, recalled:

> They used the same method of marking the route as had been used in Normandy. Behind the leading troop came a tape laying party which laid a trail of white mine tape. This marked the route of the leading formation like a paper chase. 6 Troop, under Major Leaphard, led the way in a purposeful arrowhead formation, in three blobs [sections] of twenty men in single file.

The rest of the Brigade simply followed the tape into Wesel, with German prisoners co-opted into carrying some of the commando's equipment. During this move it was important to avoid contact with the enemy, with whom they may well have become fixed in battle and, consequently, delay the whole operation or, worse, be caught out in the open at first light.

Even though they were trying to avoid contact, when observed, they had to deal with the enemy. *En route* across the open flood plain to the city, Major Leaphard came under fire from a strongly defended flak position. He attacked straight of the route of march and cutting through the perimeter wire, his men killed or captured all the gun crews. With the enemy dealt with, he then led his troop straight into the city via its north west corner before midnight, 'through an arch of contorted and buckled railway lines'.

### Into Wesel
No. 6 Commando secured an entry point just beyond the smashed railway embankment. Lieutenant Colonel Lewis received the Distinguished Service Order for this action. His citation summarised the action.

> Speed was the vital factor in this operation, as it was necessary to enter the city as soon as possible after the bombing. This was achieved largely by the skill and daring displayed by Lt-Col Lewis who led his troops with such dash that three

*separate platoon localities were quickly overrun on his way to the city. His entry into the city itself in spite of considerable opposition from small arms and Panzerfausts was affected so quickly that the remainder of the Brigade was enabled to consolidate before the enemy became aware of the situation. Lt-Col Lewis was at all times at the head of his troops, and his trust and courage contributed largely to the success of the whole operation.*

Off the flood plain and into the city the ground changed totally. One commando described the scene that greeted them:

*The streets were unrecognisable from our briefing material and many of the buildings were mere mounds of rubble. Huge craters abounded and into these flowed water mains and sewers, accompanied by escapes of flaming gas. We were held up in one street because the two leading scouts found great difficulty in making their way between a crater and one of the buildings. It took some minutes before a better route was found further to the right. The scene was well illuminated for the ensuing battle in the streets by the many fires that blazed on all sides. Despite the heavy bombing the Germans were alert and came out of the*

**One of the few surviving period houses in Rees. This example is on the outskirts.**

**Ruins and rubble of the Wesel battlefield.**

*cellars to fight with a courage and perseverance which did them great credit. The air was full of smoke and dust which was like breathing a particularly nauseous fog.*

Meanwhile, by midnight No. 45 Commando and No. 3 Commando, were following the white mine tape, with 46 abandoning its bridgehead on the riverbank once the wounded had been evacuate and bringing up the rear. The amphibious Weasels that the Brigade Commander had demanded proved their worth, being used to evacuated the wounded. The Commando Brigade and medical detachments left the riverbank just in time as a deluge of shells fell on their vacated position but having been spotted, the commandos suffered further casualties from artillery fire during crossing the open ground to Wesel.

Behind No. 6 Commando, in the order of march were the Royal Marines of 45 Commando, under 'Lieutenant Colonel Gray, who was following up rapidly behind the leading unit who had broken into the city, he passed through and debouched into the streets'. The commandos fought their way through the rubble towards the factory on the northern edge of the city.

Lieutenant Bryan Samain of E Troop 45 Commando RM describes the scene:

> We advanced in single file along both sides of a main street running north, which we hoped would bring us to our final positions. There were a lot of supposedly dead Germans lying about here, and just as Colonel Gray and his headquarters party neared the corner of the street to turn north for the wire factory – our final position – a 'dead' German (we later identified him as belonging to the SS) suddenly rose to his feet and fired a Panzerfaust at point-blank range. The result of this sudden onslaught was that two of the headquarters' men were killed, Colonel Gray wounded in the arm, and nearly everyone in the immediate vicinity knocked off their feet by the force of the explosion.
>
> Feeling very angry, we emptied a magazine of Tommy gun bullets into the German soldier, and into every subsequent 'corpse', we saw lying around.

The loss of their commanding officer at a crucial moment would have been severe. As recorded in his DSO citation:

> In spite of his wound he refused to be evacuated and completed his important task. Having captured the factory he disposed his troops so skilfully that during the next thirty-six hours they were able to beat off three major counter-attacks by infantry and self-propelled guns with enormous casualties to the enemy. Not until the last counter-attack had been broken, did

**The factory area along Wesel's northern edge looking over 45 Commando's position.**

*this gallant officer allow himself to be evacuated.*

At about 0200 hours, 45 Commando reached their objective and an hour later, were consolidating their positions around the wire factory on the north east corner of the city. Much to their amusement, they discovered the 'Wire' factory actually manufactured lavatory pans. Their commanding officer, through he was suffering considerably from the pain of his wounded arm, deployed and encouraged his men, 'who were inspired by his example'.

Lieutenant Bryan Samain and the men of his section of E Troop were immediately at work.

> *As soon as we got inside the factory, we set to work feverishly to barricade it as much as possible. Machinery, timber, doors, benches, coils of wire – all were used in an effort to prepare rough defensive positions, blocking windows and the like until they were mere loopholes... . We stood-to throughout the night waiting for an enemy counter-attack that never came.*

Lieutenant Colonel Lewis chose a house for No. 6 Commando's headquarters and 'going down to a cellar I found seventeen Germans down there, all lying on their bunks. There was no sort of control or command at this stage'. He commented that 'These people fought as individuals'.

Lieutenant Colonel Peter Bartholomew's No. 3 Commando had been last to cross the river using the Buffalo ferry but followed 45 into Wesel. Taking a more westerly route, No. 3. See map on page 111 Commando promptly found themselves clearing barricades and attacking defenders who were coming to life in the smoking ruins of Wesel.

46 Commando, bringing up the rear from the bridgehead, took up a position between No. 3 and No. 45 RM Commandos. Thus deployed, the Brigade held the north and north-western outskirts of Wesel and were well positioned to be able to repel enemy counter-attacks and to clear the remainder of the town after dawn. However, the commandos may have secured their objectives but Mills-Roberts wanted to adopt an aggressive posture. He wrote, 'While the commandos were digging-in, offensive patrols scoured the immediate area and brushes with the enemy were frequent'.

The result of one of these patrols was recorded by the Brigade Commander:

> *Major-General Deutch, the German Garrison Commander,*

*was found by a patrol of 6 Commando in his headquarters in a cellar. He refused to surrender and was killed by a burst of Tommy gun fire. In his headquarters was a map giving full details of the flak dispositions of the whole area. It was invaluable because next day the 18th Airborne Corps, American and British, was to fly in and before that time it would be possible to get our own artillery on to the German flak positions to hammer them and do as much damage as possible.*

What Mills-Roberts does not mention is that Deutch, who was actually commander of 16th Flak Division, as well as garrison commander, had his HQ located in a cellar almost next door to the building where he had established his own tactical HQ. There is also evidence that General Deutch died in more interesting circumstances when he was encountered by a 6 Commando patrol led by RSM Woodcock. Private Prichard recalled how:

*In a garden area of Wesel, a Lance Corporal was digging a grave. This seemed strange and we asked him why. It appears that he was one of RSM Woodcock's patrol searching through the cellars when he was confronted by a German officer. The Lance Corporal immediately said 'Hands up!' whereupon the German replied, 'I am General von Deutsch and I only surrender to an officer of equal rank'. The Lance Corporal is supposed to have*

**Targeting information was essential if full use was to be made of the mass of artillery such as this 5.5 inch gun.**

*said, 'This will equalise you,' and fired his Thompson at him
with fatal results. The story was that the Brigadier was furious
and ordered the Lance Corporal to bury the General as a
punishment.*

*The Lance Corporal concluded his story by commenting
'That's the last time I kill a General'.*

RSM Woodcock took numerous maps from the German
headquarters, which proved to be marked with detailed
locations of the flak batteries. To ensure that this vital
information reached XII Corps' Artillery Intelligence Cell, the
best swimmer in the Brigade was called for to take the map back
across the Rhine in a sealed package. However, the gunner radio
nets were working well:

*Ted Ruston, my Gunner representative from the Mountain
Regiment, was standing by to pass all the information over the
R.A. signal net, and our own signallers were ready to pass it
over their own net – but it would necessarily be a long and
detailed message.*

Other prisoners were being brought into Brigade Headquarters,
which was 'in a cellar, with a low archaic catacomb of pillars, lit
by dozens of candles provided by the enemy'. Here Mills-
Roberts received the surrender of a German colonel:

*There was a slight commotion as he went on his way into
captivity. He made the fatal mistake of asking Arthur de Jonghe*

123

*to assist him with his bag. Arthur, in fluent German, advised him that as a member of the Master Race he should be well able to deal with any minor impedimenta, which included a bag. The colonel looked embarrassed and unhappy and I was not sorry to see him go.*

The *Oberst* was added to the mounting number of prisoners and was directed to a large crater near Brigade Headquarters where the PoWs had been gathered in order to control them and give them some cover.

Lieutenant Samain recalled, after a sleepless night that:

*When dawn broke the next morning Easy Troop were 'standing-to' in their positions, which lay in the right-hand corner of the factory, facing east. There was still nothing happening: it seemed, in fact, as if all would be quiet, and that the airborne troops would have nothing at all to worry about ...*

*Suddenly a marine, looking out of his loophole, saw a dozen rather weary German soldiers wheeling cycles down the road leading back to the town. They were heading straight for the factory. Everyone in the troop waited for them to come closer, their weapons at the ready.*

**Siegfried Waldenburg commander *116th Panzer Division*.**

*The Germans obviously thought that, wherever the British were they were certainly not in the lavatory pan factory. They chatted amongst themselves quite unsuspectingly as they came towards the men of Easy Troop, all of whom were now in the aim, awaiting orders to open fire.*

*A few minutes later, the Germans passed within a few feet of Easy Troop: but we held our fire. Then as the last German presented his back we opened. After thirty seconds, there were twelve corpses lying in the road.*

The situation did not remain favourable for long, as by 0500 hours, it was obvious to the Germans that Wesel, in the centre of the Allied bridgehead, was their key terrain and that this was the main crossing. Consequently, *XLVII Panzer Korps* was ordered to counter-attack with all available resources. Shortly after dawn, at 0530

**By 1945 the bicycle was a common means of mobility for Germany's last reserves.**

hours the enemy were reported arriving north of the town for the expected counter-attack and before long, there was the sound of tracked vehicles and engines. Brigadier Mills Roberts wrote:

> This report came from each of the four Commandos and we asked for map references. The map references were supported by approximate compass bearings: curiously enough these bearings all crossed in the vicinity of a small copse where several roads joined, making it a likely place for armour to concentrate, ...

> When this had been verified Ted Ruston said, 'We've still got the Corps artillery on call for a bit yet. Shall we give them a pasting?' 'Yes,' I said. 'If we can deter this suspected counter – attack it's going to make quite a difference.'

> He laid on the shoot with all speed and a very satisfactory noise followed in due course.

The armoured attack failed to materialise, which is not entirely surprising when one considers the weight of fire provided by a heavy battery (7.2" guns), two medium regiments and two field regiments of 3 AGRA along with the guns of the mountain

Particularly well-equipped *Hitlerjugend* soldiers in 1945 armed with *panzerfausts*.

artillery.

As daylight came, further patrols were sent out to scour the town for centres of enemy resistance and according to the Brigadier, 'small battles were taking place everywhere in the streets'. Both sides used *Panzerfausts* as an anti-personnel weapon in the absence of tanks in these sharp, if a little one-sided fights.

> We also had a number of these weapons which were proving more destructive than accurate. One man was missed by one of these Panzerfausts and, to his amazement, saw a large slice of the building behind him collapse.

## Communications

As the commandos were not forming a permanent bridgehead on the riverbank they had not had the opportunity to tow a telephone line across the river as the infantry brigades had been able to do. To ensure communications, as radios were a tenuous link, with battle damage, running out of batteries and jamming just a few of the potential problems, a line was needed from Wesel back to the home bank. This was to be the task of Lieutenant Christie (Royal Signals), the Lines Officer of 1 Commando Brigade Signal Troop. The line was to 'be laid at the earliest possible moment' and was considered to be an 'extremely hazardous task'.

As soon as the Brigade's initial objective had been captured and a tactical HQ established, Christie took a small hand-picked line party through the city to the demolished railway bridge. At this point, of course, Wesel had not been completely cleared of the enemy and the line party had to work in full view of the enemy, including a machine-gun post sited upstream on the east bank of the river.

Lieutenant Christie's Military Cross citation reads:

*Ordering his small party to pay out the line, Lieut Christie commenced climbing across the twisted bridge spans carrying the line with him. At times he had to climb over girders 100 feet above the river while at other times he picked his path along spans which were partly submerged in the water.*

*The pull on the quadruple cable whenever it touched the water was tremendous, nevertheless by sheer courage and determination, Lieutenant Christie crossed the full 1,500-ft. length of the demolished bridge under heavy shell fire and spasmodic sniping and machine gun fire, and thus enabled vital communication to be established before the first pontoon bridge had been commenced. This officer's devotion to duty and complete disregard for his own safety was an inspiration to all who witnessed it.*

The line link was duly established and despite needing almost constant repair, provided a speedy method of passing information until the town was secured and the bridges built.

## Counter-Attack

The most dangerous period for 1 Commando Brigade was as expected, at 1000 hours, when the copious artillery support from the home bank that the assault formations had hitherto used liberally, had to be checked for three and a half hours during the airborne operation. Unfortunately, this coincided with the likely arrival time of German operational reserves, in the form of armoured counter-attacks. In the seven hours available to them, when not patrolling, the commandos had done their best to dig-in or build sangars in the piles of rubble and had gathered as many *panzerfausts* as possible from prisoners and defended locations to make up for the lack of their own anti-tank weapons.

As predicted, the pressure against 1 Commando Brigade mounted, just as the artillery check fire came into force. The enemy was a *Kampfgruppe* of *116th Windhund Panzer Division*, consisting of infantry supported by assault guns. This was one of the battle groups that had been held back to counter-attack Allied bridgeheads on the Rhine. Harried by fighter-bombers they had only been able to concentrate in the woods and copses north of Wesel, slowly and with losses to both men and armour. Hitherto, the fire of the Mountain Regiment, supplemented by that of the Army Group's Royal Artillery, had disrupted the enemy's assembly but now with further troops arriving the main weight of the attack fell on 45 Commando who struggled to keep the enemy at bay. Waves of grenadiers, supported by *Panzer IVs* and assault guns, attacked the commandos. Concentrated fire from Bren guns and other small arms fire, however, halted the German infantry assaults and, according to German sources, the attack principally failed because the *Panzers* were overly cautious. Presumably, deterred by the presence of Allied fighter-bombers and even medium bombers in cab ranks above the battlefield. Also, they would have been

**A Vickers machine gun was the heaviest weapon that the Brigade possessed at Wesel.**

**A *Waffen* SS soldier operating a *Panzerschrek*.**

at a considerable disadvantage if they had attempted to fight amongst the rubble of the town.

45 Commando's historian recalled that with the check fire period in force: 'The Hun chose this moment to launch a counter-attack to regain the all important factory. ... the enemy was able to advance across the open ground with infantry and tanks supported by his own sporadic mortar fire'. Colonel Gray without artillery support or other heavy weapons ordered that all PIATs should be used in the unusual 'mortar' role. Angled up, these weapons had a range of some three hundred yards – 'at the receiving end, the effect was very similar to that of an artillery barrage'.

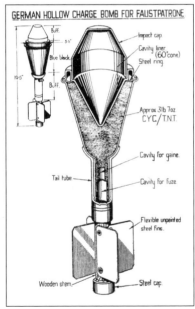

GERMAN HOLLOW CHARGE BOMB FOR FAUSTPATRONE

Lieutenant Samain recalled:

> ... It was not until 1000 hours that they put in their first organised counter-attack; and when it came it seemed to be a

*most half-hearted affair, consisting of a few waves of infantry, supported by cumbersome Mark IV tanks and self propelled guns. The infantry were easily beaten off, and for some unknown reason the tanks did not attempt to come too close.*

*There were in fact two really serious attempts to dislodge us later in the day. The first was when a solitary Mark IV, braver than its fellows, started to rumble ominously down the main road towards us. It got to within one hundred and fifty yards of the factory, then became indecisive. Major Beadle, meanwhile had mustered every available PIAT and Panzerfaust, and these were ready. Suddenly, however, the tank stopped, its engines coughing and arguing, then turned around and went back. Discretion being the better part of valour, Easy Troop let it go.*

Lance Corporal John Sykes of B Troop 45 Commando RM had an altogether more difficult battle, and received the Military Medal for his action during the battle on 24 March. He commanded the forward Bren group sighted outside the north east corner of the wire factory. What were thought to be two 88 mm self-propelled guns approached to within 500 yards and engaged the troop position with HE and machine gun fire. His citation describes the action:

*A shell-burst four feet above his position on the wall seriously wounded his No. 2 of the Bren. He immediately assisted the medical orderly to remove the casualty and organised a relief and then engaged an enemy machine gun position 250 yards from his right front. Five minutes later another shell burst immediately in front of his trench blowing his Bren gun out of the position. Sykes again left his cover and under machine-gun fire recovered the gun, which was still serviceable, returned to his trench, and again engaged the enemy.*

*A third shell hit the wall to the left of his position, this time breaching the barrel of the gun. Sykes jumped from his trench with the damaged gun, ran to Troop HQ for the spare Bren and returned to his post and returned the enemy's fire. His aggressive spirit and determination to fight back was a shining example of courage during a most trying period...*

A little further along the line another self-propelled gun was 'sniping' at E Troop from the cover of a cemetery wall. Lieutenant Samain wrote:

*About half an hour later ... a second Mark IV approached to within 250 yards of the factory and commenced to pump shells*

The workhorse of the German army, the *Panzerkampfwagen* IV, with its 75 mm gun, served on all fronts.

The area of 45 Commando's open right flank. The railway now crossed by a road bridge was the site of a level crossing.

*into it. As it was out of PIAT range and because the artillery had been forbidden to fire during the airborne operation there was really nothing that could be done about it: so we just lay quietly under what cover we could, enduring a most unpleasant bombardment of 75-millimetre shells, until the German crew finally tired of their party games and withdrew. E Troop suffered six or seven casualties.*

45 Commando's historian considers that the decision not to bring anti-tank guns across with the Brigade, as 'there wasn't a significant tank threat', was 'extremely questionable'. Lieutenant Samain, supporting this view, commented that 'Had the Mark IVs pressed home their attack, of course, they would have caused untold damage, for our defensive positions were far from perfect, and we had nothing more than PIATs and a *Panzerfaust* or two'.

Following this incident, Major Beadle received a message from the CO that he could pull E Troop back into less exposed positions in the centre of the factory complex. However, believing that this would allow the enemy to gain a foothold in the area and that 'getting them out would be a costly business', he declined to move his troop.

At about the same time, Brigadier Mills-Roberts redeployed A Troop of No. 3 Commando to join 45 Commando, strengthening the Brigade's open flank, by covering the remains of a level crossing. Here the Army Commandos found that they were 'being pestered by enemy self-propelled guns'.

Meanwhile, a troop of 46 Commando, who were positioned in a builder's yard on the far side of the road opposite 45 had been 'conducting a small war of their own against scattered parties of Germans who were scurrying about isolated buildings in a small village three hundred yards to the east of the town'. The Commandos sniped at them throughout the morning with commendable accuracy, 'and there is no doubt at all that this largely contributed to the enemy's failure to mount a really large scale attack on them'. Every time they brought up an SP gun, or infantry started forming up in the village for a counter-attack, their arrangements were disrupted by small arms fire.

The drop of 17th US Airborne Division took place just to the north of Wesel, with the paratroopers of 3rd Battalion 507 Parachute Infantry Regiment landing on DZ W to the north

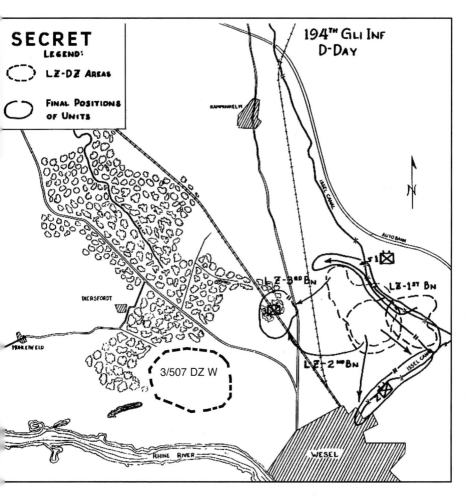

194ᵀᴴ Gʟɪ Iɴғ
D-Dᴀʏ

west of Wesel on the self-same open ground that the commandos had crossed the night before. The paratroopers were followed by the Wacos of 2nd and 3rd Battalions 194th Glider Infantry swooping in to land little more than a mile away. The dramatic arrival of the airborne in the middle of the battle caused a noticeable slackening of the Germans' resolve but due to a combination of mist, smoke and heavy flak 17th US Airborne's landing had been dispersed and they had suffered heavy casualties in landing, as planned directly on top of the enemy. Consequently it would be some time before the Glidermen whose principal objectives were the bridges on the

Issel and Issel Canal would be able to make their presence felt to the benefit of the commandos.

Colonel Gray who had been wounded during 45's initial advance into the town, eventually succumbed to the pain of his wound and was forced to hand over command to Major Blake, who in the early afternoon, reported that another enemy attack was coming in. To defeat this attack, which was getting perilously close to his position, Captain Day called for fire from the 3.7-inch guns of the Mountain Regiment, immediately in front of him. 'The response was so rapid and accurate that a badly shaken Captain Day barely had time to dive into his bunker'. The attack was beaten off.

By 1300 hours, two sizeable *kampfgruppen* were forming up east and north-east of 45 RM Commando's position, supported by self-propelled guns. Brigadier Mills-Roberts recalled:

*We arranged an artillery programme with Ted Ruston but they would not be able to fire before 1.30 p.m. – till then we*

*would have to manage with small – arms fire as no mortars were allowed either.*

*At 1.30 p.m. down came the long-awaited artillery support, which we had been unable to get till the Airborne troops were all in. Less than half an hour later the battle in No. 45's area was well under control.*

This is a graphic example of the power of artillery to swing a battle and the Brigadier considered that this was 'the turning point of the whole battle and now I felt that the brigade was secure in Wesel'.

At about 1700 hours, patrols from 2nd Battalion 194th Glider Infantry of 17th US Airborne Division entered the Brigade position through the forward troops of 45 Commando and passed on details of their dispositions along the Issel Canal. At this stage, these were the only patrols that had infiltrated across no-man's-land and through German-held ground. A proper link up was not made until the following day. However, the presence of the American Glidermen to the north east, did much to prevent the Germans from attacking the Commando Brigade's defences on the northern perimeter. Consequently, with the situation on the northern outskirts of the town more or less under control, Brigadier Mills-Roberts was able to progressively increase the number of men clearing the town's central area.

### The Clearance and Occupation of Wesel
While the battle on the northern edge of the town had been going on, 6 Troop of No. 6 Commando had been tasked to secure a bridgehead on the river bank at the opposite end of Wesel, through which, the Brigade would be reinforced and resupplied. At about 1300 hours they reported that they had cleared the bank of the Rhine in the area of the blown railway bridge. Shortly afterwards Brigade HQ ordered the LVT ferry to be opened, at 1420 hours, at a site upstream side of the demolished bridge.

There was, however, a delay passing the order to 81 Field Company RE and the first Buffalo, carrying an RE recce party, crossed without incident at 1500 hours. The site had been chosen from air photographs and in the end proved to be too steep for Buffaloes. To make matters worse, the ferry site promptly came under fire from a *spandau* in the uncleared part of the town. One Buffalo was holed and sank at the foot of the

194 US Glider
Infantry Regt

WESEL

46
Cmdo

3
Cmdo

45
Cmdo

6
Cmdo

1 Cheshire Regt

Barracks

Actual

Intended

Fusternberg

30 US Divisi

ramp, blocking it. By 1600 hours, however, an alternative landing site was located just downstream of the bridge.

Meanwhile, 1 Cheshire, the spare battalion of 115 Brigade that was not providing Bank Control Parties for the two assaulting corps, came under command of the Commando Brigade. At 1400 hours, the two commanders of A and B Companies were briefed and shortly afterwards the Battalion left its assembly area in trucks but as the leading vehicle approached the river the column came under fire from a *spandau* and the column was halted. It is reported that:

> *Mortars of 4/5 Royal Scots Fusiliers laid a smoke screen and put down HE on the enemy position, which was neutralised so that the trucks could proceed back to the Battalion area to pick up the remainder of the troops.*

The ferrying of A and B Companies began at about 1600 hours and the only enemy reaction was intermittent firing by the *spandau*, which was again temporarily neutralised by mortars of 4/5 RSF. The Cheshires crossed the Rhine without casualties but it was found that the Battalion's Jeeps and carriers could not be landed at the new ferry site. As a result, A and B Companies moved inland without waiting for them at 1700 hours. As they moved towards their objective, the *spandau* again came to life and one soldier was wounded and evacuated. No further resistance was encountered and by 1730 hours, both Companies were digging themselves in the north west portion of the green belt in Wesel along with their Tactical HQ.

At 1800 hours, C and D Companies crossed and moved inland. The *spandau* that had caused problems earlier was still firing and a second machine gun in the area also opened up, but without causing any casualties to the Cheshires. On the bank, there were still anti-personnel mines and a Sergeant Major was wounded by a *Schumine*. By 1830 hours, the two companies had reached the south side of the railway embankment and were digging in. The Battalion's main HQ crossed the river at 1900 hours and joined Tac HQ in the cellar of a house in the battalion area. The Cheshires reported:

> *Thus, by 1900 hours 1 CHESHIRE, less Support Company*

*and all the vehicles, had crossed the Rhine and settled for the night in slit trenches and cellars. A firm belt from the river to the 6 Commando bridgehead was held and the supply route to the Commandos was secure. Enemy activity had been limited to intermittent firing from one, and in the later stages two, machine guns and a small amount of shelling and a few AP mines. There was no contact with the enemy on the ground, except that two Germans surrendered to the battalion.*

The bombing, the arrival of the commandos and the moral effect of the airborne drop had together totally dislocated the enemy who were not capable of putting up an organised defence.

The difficulty that the Cheshires had with the pair of *spandaus* was replicated on the opposite side of Wesel, where small arms artillery and mortar fire seriously delayed ferrying and bridging operations by 30th US Infantry Division. This was to cause a delay which, in circumstances other than the almost complete collapse of the 180th Grenadier Division, could have been

**The Cheshires finally ashore west of the blown bridge at Wesel.**

138

**British troops escorting a column of prisoners.**

serious. As it was, *116th Panzer Division*, committed to battle piecemeal, to stem the tide of the Allied advance, was easily held.

While the Cheshires were crossing and occupying the southern portion of Wesel, A Troop of 3 Commando who had been released from their earlier task of reinforcing 45 Commando with the arrival of the Americans, were now clearing their way into the centre of the town. Fighting in light battle order, using No. 38 radio sets for communication, they ambushed several German patrols working their way north through the rubble and developed a technique for dealing with enemy riflemen who wished to fight on, which involved drawing fire and then concentrating several Brens on the snipers' position.

Elements of No. 6 Commando who were now fighting in the town were also facing some determined resistance:

> One patrol reported that when a number of the enemy had approached them in apparent surrender, one of them dropped down on his hands and knees with a spandau strapped to his back. The patrol were the ones to return so they must have

The German barrack area across the railway from 45 Commando's position.

Troops of 30th US Division on the east bank of the Rhine near Wesel.

*reacted swiftly.*

46 Commando RM eventually pushed through the town to link up with the Cheshires, who had deployed to clear and defend the south west part of the town. With pressure from the east reducing, they were able to assist with the aggressive patrolling operations in the main part of the town, where a smoky haze hung over Wesel 'that got into one's nostrils and eyes'.

No. 3 Commando had cleared the centre of the town by late afternoon and Brigade HQ reported the town clear during the evening of 24 March but this is considered 'to have been a little premature' by Second Army, as there were a few pockets of resistance still holding and disrupting movement in and around the city.

The following day (25 March), firm contact was made with 507 Parachute Infantry, to the north west of the town, at 1330 hours. With the link-up made, 1 Commando Brigade was passed from command of XII Corps to that of XVIII US Airborne Corps, for subsequent operations.

In this final phase of the battle, as planned, 45 Commando was to clear a German barrack area to the south east of their position. B Troop was ordered to send out a patrol to clear some houses on the far side of the railway prior to the attack on the barracks, which was one of the last bastions of resistance.

*The patrol commander, Lt McDonald, with his section cleared the first buildings without difficulty, but further progress was checked by the Germans who were still occupying strong defences near their barracks. The patrol was withdrawn when it was discovered that this phase of the operation was to be undertaken by US Paratroopers. B and D Troops had a ringside seat for the attack by the US paras supported by British self-propelled guns [Archers].*

Later in the afternoon of 25 March, 46 Commando reported a link-up with troops of the Ninth US Army astride the Lippe Canal, south of the town. The clearance of the town was finally completed at 2100 hours and the Commandos were able to 'sample the contents of captured hock barrels'.

As a result of the bombing and fighting to clear Wesel, the town had been 'reduced to a mass of rubble, twisted girders and beams, smouldering fires and precariously balanced walls verging on collapse'. The total number of prisoners taken was over eight hundred and fifty: several hundred enemy lay dead

**A Commando patrol combing the ruins for enemy resistance.**

by their slit trenches on the flood plain and in the streets of Wesel. In contrast, commando casualties totalled ninety-seven killed, wounded and missing.

Before leaving 1 Commando Brigade in Wesel, it is worth noting that the large town of Wesel was captured as rapidly as could be expected, and cleared to enable bridging operations by Ninth United States Army to commence. Whereas the smaller town of Rees, which was not attacked by bombers immediately before the assault, was the scene of severe fighting that lasted for over forty-eight hours.

# CHAPTER 6

# Operation TORCHLIGHT
# 15th (Scottish) Division

THE SECOND ARMY'S Operation PLUNDER's main effort lay with XII Corps. In their crossing of the Rhine, XII Corps' intention was, with or without the drop of XVIII US Airborne Corps, to force a crossing of the Rhine, seize the Issel bridges (if not captured by 6th Airborne), establish ferries and eventually bridge the Rhine. From the resulting lodgement, the Corps was to be prepared to operate eastwards into the heart of Germany.

To this end, a Mobile Striking Force based on an armoured regiment and an infantry battalion mounted in Kangaroo armoured personnel carriers, was to be given the highest priority on the ferries and was to be ready for operations by first light on D+2.

Leading XII Corps' assault was 15th (Scottish) Division. Their crossing was to take place at 0200 hours on 24 March, some five hours after the attack by 51st Highland Division and four hours after that of 1 Commando Brigade. The crossing was timed to be coordinated with that of the crossing of XVI US Corps to their right (Operation FLASHLIGHT).

Lieutenant General Ritchie, commander of XII Corps.

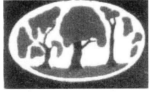

XII Corps' shoulder flash.

15th Scottish Division.

### Enemy Forces

XII Corps, although they were unsure of the exact enemy boundaries, knew that their assault area was opposite elements

of 7th *Fallschirmjäger* Division and 84th Infantry Division, both of which, as already discussed were shadows of their former selves. However, in prepared positions they were still expected to give a good account of themselves against the vulnerable Scottish infantry advancing across the river and open flood plain. It was known that the defenders in the 84th Division area now included not only *Volkssturm* but also, for example, *280 (Ear) Battalion*, which was made up of soldiers who were deaf or hard of hearing. These reinforcements on the face of it seem to have been of a very low quality but similar troops had performed surprisingly well during the battle of the Bulge and of course during VERITABLE, when they had already faced 15th Scottish Division.

**Generalmajor** Fiebig commander 84th Division.

An estimate of enemy artillery that XII Corps could face made by gunner intelligence was that:

> *84th Inf Div assisted by GHQ and non-divisional resources, was thought to have only about fifty medium guns: in fact there were probably more, and they were in any case very difficult to*

**Panzerwerfer** 150 mm ten-barrelled rocket mortar the *nebelwerfer.*

*locate, as they were mostly sited in very enclosed country. To this figure must be added the guns which 7 Para Div might bring to bear against 12 Corps.*

This total did not include the more manoeuvrable and even more difficult to locate, medium mortars and *Nebelwerfers* which were, throughout the North West European Campaign, the weapon system that inflicted the greatest casualties amongst the Allies.

### 15th Division's Training and Preparations

The two formations of the 15th Scottish Division selected to spearhead the assault across the Rhine, were the 44 Lowland and the 227 Highland Brigades. These two formations were programmed to carry out two full-scale practice crossings on the River Maas (Exercise BUFFALO):

*... the first, a daylight exercise on 14th March; the second, a night exercise on 15 March.*

*Under command for this exercise the 15th Scottish Division had the following formations and units, which were to remain under it until it crossed the Rhine: the 4th Armoured Brigade, of which the 44th Royal Tanks were equipped with DD Tanks (Shermans), fitted with water-wings and propellers which enabled them to swim under their own power; the 11th Army Group R.E. (A.G.R.E.); an S.P. Anti-Tank Battery; and a 'Bank Group,' composed of signals, medical, recovery, and traffic control sub-units grouped round the 5th Royal Berkshire [115 Brigade]. For the exercise, as for the real crossing, two squadrons of the Royal Dragoons and about fifty officers from Reinforcement Holding Units were given to the Royal Berkshire in addition. The Bank Group thus disposed of about a hundred officers – enough to allow for an officer at every small control-post. This Bank Group was to function in much the same way as a Beach Group and to control the forward passage of troops, vehicles, and stores across the river obstacle.*

The Division had in support, as was usual for any major operation, Hobart's Funnies attached from 33 Armoured Brigade. Besides the two squadrons of DDs, there were the usual flails, Crocodiles, and Kangaroos, for the later stages of the operation. There were of course two regiments, 11 Royal Tank Regiment (11 RTR) and the East Riding Yeomanry, both equipped with LVT Buffaloes. The historian of 2 Argyll and

**Loading of a carrier, the largest vehicle that the Buffalo could carry during training on the Maas.**

Sutherland Highlanders commented:

> *The yeomanry responsible for the actual crossing were a delightful lot to work with, with a fine cavalry dash and a persistently horsey outlook, even in the water, when the squadron commanders were heard urging their drivers to 'get their whips out'.*

**Royal Tank Regiment**
**East Riding Yeomanry**

The marshalling of all these troops during the daylight exercise was a success but the night exercise was conducted 'in the worst possible conditions of fog and darkness. Much went wrong in consequence, but the snags that had been revealed were duly dealt with after the post-mortem'. Exercise over and no opportunity for a re-run, the even more complicated process of concentrating the Division on the Rhine began. The LVT loading tables were almost as complicated as those of the Normandy D Day, with infantry companies having to give up a specified number of places on their six Buffaloes to members of the Bank Group and other specialists who were needed across the river as soon as possible.

146

## 15th Division's Plan

Major General Barber's task was, on a two brigade frontage, to establish a bridgehead between Bislich and Vynen, 'preparatory to securing the area of Bergerfurth along with its bridge', which is referred to as Bridge A. This bridge was important, as the old course of the Rhine was, in effect, a second obstacle or potential line of resistance to be crossed before the Scots could reach 6th Airborne Division in the area of Hamminkeln. If not already secured, 15th Division was to go on and capture the bridges over the Issel. No less than six field regiments, four medium regiments, two heavy AA batteries and a pair of heavy or super heavy batteries would support each of the assault brigades. The crushing weight of fire delivered by these guns would be supplemented by those of the remainder of the Army Group's Royal Artillery in the case of emergency. The apogee of the British artillery's power was the 'Pepperpot', where all available guns were concentrated in an annihilating strike against specific targets, built into the general fire plan to maximise effect on key points.

See map on page 148

5.5 British artillery piece on the west bank of the Rhine lays down covering fire.

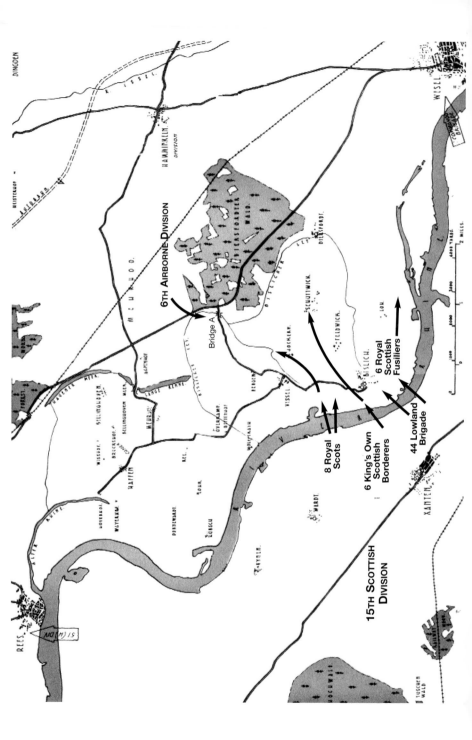

148

An important part of Major General Barber's plan included 100 Anti-Aircraft Brigade. In addition to its normal role of protecting the ferry and bridging sites from enemy aircraft, this brigade was also to provide river security by coordinating the efforts to prevent the Germans from destroying the crossing sites and bridges with mines and divers swimming downstream.

### 44 Lowland Brigade – Codeword POKER

On the Division's right flank, the Lowland Brigade was to cross the Rhine and capture and hold the area Schuttwick, Loh and Bislich. 11 RTR were to lift the two assault battalions, with 6 Royal Scots Fusiliers (6 RSF) being right assault and 8 Royal Scots (8 RS) left. Their initial objectives were to clear the line of the Bund immediately west of Bislich, between Fahrhaus and Ronduit and to occupy the western half of Bislich. Thereafter, 6 King's Own Scottish Borderers (6 KOSB) was then to pass through 6 RSF and seize the remainder of Bislich, after which the whole brigade was to advance north and east to the Diersfordterwald, where it was anticipated they would link up with the British and American airborne troops.

See map on page 150

With news circulating of the success of the initial crossing by fellow Scots in 51st Highland Division to their north and the Commandos just to their east, 'soon after midnight 23 / 24 March the assaulting battalions embarked in their allotted LVTs in the Marshalling Area'. The divisional historian explained that the planning staff had allocated:

> ... six LVT to an infantry company, with a further twelve per battalion carrying Bn HQ and supporting weapons, including detachments of medium machine guns of 1st Battalion, Middlesex Regiment (1 MX). In addition, the assault wave LVTs carried RA Observation Parties, advanced parties of the Bank Group (5 Berks) including medical personnel, RE and DD reconnaissance parties.

> ... a proportion of LVT had been loaded with the minimum vehicles essential in the assault stages of the operation. The stowage of LVTs in the assault waves had been worked out in detail by HQ XII Corps and though there was some slight variation between battalions, the following allotment of vehicles was generally adopted:

> 6-pounder A/Tk guns and towers, 4
> Jeeps 3 (one each for CO, medical officer, RE recce officer), 4

**Typically heavily laden infantry mounting LVTs in the assembly area.**

> *Carriers (two for reserve ammunition and one each for the RA OP party and battalion signal officer).*

Under the cover of the sound of fighting to the flanks and their own 'Pepperpot' barrage falling on the opposite bank the two regiments of Buffaloes each set out for the river, in a single file, at 0330 hours. Lieutenant Peter White recalled that 'One felt a sense of privilege at being present as another milestone of history was heaved slowly and massively into position for its unveiling in the coming hours.' And then at 0155 hours '... waves of tightly packed Buffaloes roared, squeaking their way through gaps blown by the REs in the dyke wall to splash towards their objectives.' Here 'the columns paused momentarily ... to check timings, and then the first flights, comprising three companies per assaulting battalion, passed

**BBC reporter, Wynford Vaughan Thomas, was recording a live report in one of the Buffaloes.**

through the gaps, fanned out into line and entered the water' at H Hour (0200 hours).

BBC reporter, Wynford Vaughan Thomas, was recording a live report in one of the Buffaloes:

*The driver feels for the edge of the water – we're guided up right to the very edge by a long line of small green lights that have been laid to take us to the jumping-off ground: we've reached the water's edge and we see the Rhine – not running, as we thought it would, bright under the moon, but running red; because right on the opposite side of the village every single house and haystack you can see is burning, beaten down by the fury of our barrage. We can't tell whether there's anything coming at our boys: we hope all the stuff that we hear is going into Germany.*

The Buffaloes, having been carried downstream to the approximate area of their proposed landing, headed for the bank and started to climb out of the river. At this point, it was intended that the soldiers would be led into battle by a battalion piper. Wynford Vaughan Thomas was aboard an LVT with the Commanding Officer of 6 RSF (the battalion commanded by Winston Churchill in the Great War), who:

*... gave the signal, the piper lifted his pipes to his lips, and he blew, and only an agonised wailing came from his instrument. Again he tried, and again the wail. If ever a man was near to tears, it was our piper. His great moment, and now, as he cried in despair 'Ma pipes, man, they'll no play.'*

Battalion records, however, show that Piper McGhee played the regiment march Cutty's Wedding. The piper recalled 'There was nothing to it, but I was a bit scared when I first boarded the Buffalo. There was a good deal of sniping and mortar fire, but the actual crossing wasn't too bad.'

The leading companies were all across on time, around dawn, having disembarked 'dry shod'. There was some desultory shelling and mortaring and both 6 RSF and 8 RS

Bislich

Rhine

Dyke Road

**Three defended houses on the dyke overlooking 8th Royal Scots' crossing point. The centre house was used as their tactical HQ for some time.**

reported 'a certain amount of trouble from light automatic fire'. On the Brigade's left flank, 8 Royal Scots made a good landing on the east bank, having, according to the Adjutant, Captain Fargus:

> Spasmodic mortar and shellfire was directed at the LVTs as they approached the river and during the crossing, some very inaccurate Spandau fire was opened. This caused no casualties and the crossing was accomplished without incident.

The Royals crossed the river in three waves at four minute intervals, with each wave heading for their own landfall. A and B Companies led off from their drop off point and took their objectives without great difficulty, 'although some of the *Spandau* posts dug in on the farther side of the dyke defended themselves stubbornly, having suffered little damage from our artillery bombardment'.

C Company met the fiercest opposition and had great difficulty in overcoming one particular resolute post. The company commander and another officer became casualties. Soon all the rifle companies were on their objectives and 'patrols were sent out to clean up any enemy who might be lying up in houses or entrenched in their respective areas'.

D Company sent a platoon to B Company's area to allow B Company to extend to Gossenhof farm, which was captured after a sharp fight with a group of enemy, including an artillery

154

OP party, who were all either killed or captured. The Adjutant, Captain Fargus, was holding the prisoners of war near Battalion Headquarters in the cover of the dyke:

> *Isolated* Spandau *posts dug in on the slopes of the bund, gave some trouble. As anticipated, all the prisoners came from 84th Infantry Division, except for one soldier whose* soldbuch *showed a formation unknown to the intelligence officer. The mystery was solved when he stated that he was on leave from the Eastern Front, and had no intention of fighting on the Rhine.*

> *...8 RS completed Phase 1 of the operation without great difficulties. No mines were met in the flood bed as had been feared and the initial objective around the Ronduit Bridge and track junction were taken.*

Meanwhile, on the right flank, 6 RSF sustained casualties from anti-personnel mines around the ferry jetty and suffered significant casualties in D Company, when two British heavy shells fell short.

Major Bokenham, Officer Commanding D Company, described the action once he and his men were ashore:

> *Our objective was a bund 500 yards inland, but to gain it we had to cross a nearer and smaller bund, a road, and then move up between a narrow orchard on the left and a small wood on the right. The Buffaloes took us about 75 yards inland, when they came under* Spandau *and rifle fire from the nearer bund. Immediately the two leading platoons leapt out and charged. On the top of the bund, they encountered two rows of barbed wire, overcame the opposition*

A farm just inland from 6 RSF's landing point that was held by the *Fallschirmjäger.*

**A 25-pounder gun crew from 15th Scottish Division firing a barrage in support of the infantry east of the river.**

*easily and took about 30 prisoners. They then pushed on to the further bund and crossed the road without casualties, although it was found later to be heavily laid with* Schumines. *They pressed on to their objective, came under fire from it, successfully assaulted and gained it, and consolidated about 75 yards apart. Just beyond this bund were three houses from which fire was being directed at the platoons. Under Lieutenant Murphy 16 Platoon quickly cleared one, while 17 Platoon under Sergeant Linard cleared the others, taking in all twenty-five prisoners.*

*Simultaneously, 18 Platoon followed up and cleared an orchard and houses on the left. Then, led by Lieutenant Binge, they passed over the bund between 17 and 16 Platoons, cleared it and linked up with C Company about 200 yards to the left; after which they went into reserve behind 16 and 17 platoons, clearing a* Spandau *post on the way and taking eighteen prisoners. D Company dug in awaiting the order to move to the intermediate objective, which was 500 yards to the right along the bund. Casualties so far had been light, but unfortunately,*

156

*Fusilier Rogers was killed, and Sergeant Bell and Fusilier Murphy wounded.*

By 0330 hours, 6 RSF's initial objectives had been taken; Major Bokenham's D Company then started its move to its intermediate position on the Brigade's right flank:

*Orders came to move to the intermediate objective at H plus 90, and exactly at that time, when the company was moving off, tragedy occurred. Two of our own artillery shells, which had been falling close for some time, dropped short and landed in the middle of two of the platoons. Casualties were high ... [three] were killed; ... [ten] were wounded.*

*It was now that the men of the company displayed their greatness. With so many casualties, two platoons were at half-strength. Corporal Crearie, the senior surviving NCO, did magnificent work in rounding up the remnants and forming them into one platoon of approximately eighteen men. Sergeant Curran, too, now commanding 16 Platoon, was stoutly rallying his men. The company thus pushed on to the intermediate objective, Corporal Crearie's platoon along enemy's side of the bund clearing all buildings, and Sergeant Curran's on the river side. This phase of the battle was completed successfully because of the fine leadership of the two new platoon commanders. The company dug in on the intermediate objective, having taken some 30 more prisoners. The only additional casualty was Fusilier Moffat, wounded.*

Even with casualties amongst the company's leadership, it was with considerable dash that the Jocks went on to clear and occupy the western outskirts of Bislich. Here they had 'a sharp hand-to-hand struggle for a house that had been converted into a strong point, which ultimately yielded some forty prisoners'. Bislich was not yet entirely under the RSF's control as 'mopping up was still continuing, some enemy parties having gone to ground in cellars'.

While D Company was moving to its objective, 'wonderful bravery was being shown by Captain Mann and the company stretcher-bearers, who were evacuating the wounded to the river's edge and thence to the regimental aid post' ... the available stretchers were quickly used up and improvised ones made. Even so, the casualties could not all be got back. Company Sergeant-Major Black and Fusilier Williams in particular distinguished themselves by making repeated journeys under small arms and artillery fire carrying wounded across on their shoulders.

Some hours earlier, when the message had come through to HQ 44 Brigade, at 0305 hours, that the leading assault companies were established ashore, Brigadier Cumming-Bruce ordered 6 KOSB to cross. They had already marched on foot down to the storm boat waiting area at Luttingen, 'where they sheltered from desultory shelling in the houses and cellars'. At 0330 hours, C and D Companies started crossing and, suffered the usual breakdowns of the unreliable storm boat engines. Eighteen-year-old Private Frederick Hambly recalled his trip across the river:

> *The noise of the battle raging overhead was terrific as we*
> *approached the area of embarkation. We, D Company, 6th Bn*

**Infantrymen of 15th Scottish Division disembarking from a storm boat after dawn on 24 March 1945.**

*KOSB embarked on our frail craft, cast off from the west bank. We were nearly halfway across when the engine cut out. We watched as our landing area on the far bank, with its white tapes denoting that that area has been cleared of mines, receded from us, as being without engine power we were swept by the strong current, broadside towards the North Sea!*

*We were however fortunate enough to be spotted by another boat returning for its second run, and its skipper manoeuvred around the stern to our port side, lashed the two boats together and steadily moved upstream to our disembarkation area.*

Despite the unreliable engines, 6 KOSB were complete on the eastern bank by 0415 hours and with the banks having been cleared of defended posts, snipers and mines, the battalion did not suffer a single casualty to enemy action during the actual crossing.

Having formed up and crossed the flood plain and the dyke, A and B Companies of the Borderers were to press on and clear the north east part of Bislich and Feldwick. Here they met some resistance put up by 1062 Grenadier Regiment but by 0700 hours, they were secure in the village

Once the KOSB were in their objective, 44 Lowland Brigade had a continuous bridgehead and the business of pushing outwards began. Captain Fargus recalled that, 'At 0700 hours, 24 March the Brigade Commander crossed the river and saw all his battalion commanders in turn. Progress was satisfactory everywhere'.

### 227 Highland Brigade – Codeword NAP
The Highland Brigade was to cross the Rhine, capture and hold the area of Haffen and Mehr. Brigadier Colville held his final coordinating conference on 22 March, to confirm the written orders issued on 18 March. His plan was to assault with two battalions, 10 Highland Light Infantry (10 HLI) on the right and 2 Argyll and Sutherland Highlanders (2 A&SH) to the left. 2 Gordon was initially in reserve, and was to cross on orders of Brigade HQ, when Overkamp and Lohr were reported clear, relieving 10 HLI and 2 A&SH respectively; the latter battalions were then to exploit to Bellinguoven and Wisshof. Once established in their bridgeheads, the two assault brigades would close the gap between them, up to their mutual boundary, while 227 Brigade would be responsible for linking

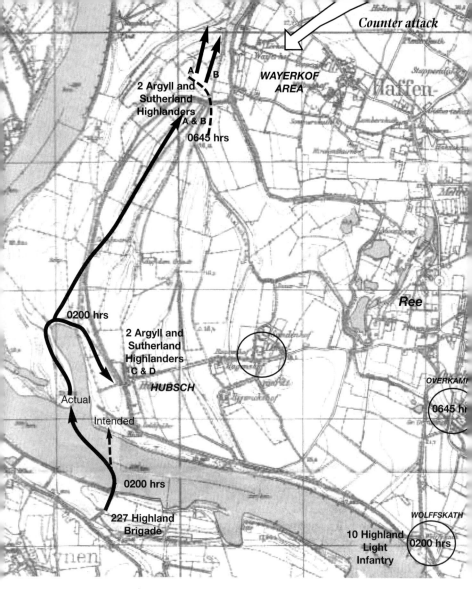

up with 52 Highland Division near Rees.

According to 10 HLI's plan made by Lieutenant Colonel Bramwell Davis:

> ... the right-hand company of the HLI, C, was to clear Wolffskath and then advance inland along the bund to Overkamp, while A Company on the left was to clear westward along the other bund that runs parallel to the river close to its edge. When A Company had reached the junction point with the

**Infantry climbing aboard a Buffalo of the East Riding Yeomanry.**

*Argylls it was to have pushed inland and cleared Ree, where it would have found itself abreast of C Company in Overkamp.*

The crossing of 227 Highland Brigade, however, did not go nearly as well as that of 44 Brigade. The leading companies of 10 HLI crossed without casualties, but were landed several hundred yards to the right, missing C Company's objective at Wolffskath, causing some confusion in the darkness and opening a wide gap between the two assault battalions. The HLI found the dyke strongly held by three companies of *1/21 Fallschirmjäger Regiment*, with a strongpoint at Wolffskath, and A Company suffered numerous casualties, including all their Company's officers while clearing it. CSM Wright took command of the Company and was justifiably awarded the DCM for his 'cool handling of the company'. According to the divisional historian:

*C Company had also pushed down-stream to Wolffskath, where it was promptly pinned by 20-mm. and LMG fire, losing*

**The view from the German held river dyke down onto the ground that the leading waves of infantry had to cross.**

> *all its officers but one. Most of the tracer was coming from the houses at Bettenhof* [on the outskirts of Overkamp], *about a thousand yards inland from Wolffskath: clearly, Bettenhof had to be cleared. The FOO's wireless was 'out,' but C Company's 18-set was still working and it passed the FOO's call for fire on Bettenhof.*

Meanwhile, B and D Companies in the second flight of the East Riding Yeomanry's LVTs, had also been landed incorrectly, resulting in 'a highly confused situation'. In the 'plan' that finally emerged from the chaos, B Company took on completing the clearance of the riverside bund and while believing that the bund had already been cleared, D Company formed up behind C to the east of the north-south bund that led to Overkamp. Matters were not helped by the absence of Battalion HQ, which had been landed too far to the right and advancing inland, was temporarily stranded in no-man's-land, where it was attacked and 'only extricated at 0500 hours with some difficulty'. That 'difficulty' included '... the complete OP party of the 131st Field Regiment, R.A., being ambushed and wiped out'.

However, the guns of the artillery finally answered the call for fire on Bettenhof:

> *Down came the concentration exactly where it was wanted, whereupon C and D Companies – totalling together much less than one company's strength – went in, in open order. They took Bettenhof together with forty-four prisoners, and there in the*

162

*southern portion of Overkamp they dug in.*

By dawn, D and C Companies were secure in the outskirts of Overkamp. At this point, the third flight of LVTs, containing most of Support Company and essential vehicles was ordered across the Rhine. Meanwhile B Company had cleared the riverside bund as far as the battalion boundary. The divisional historian recounted:

> *In front of B there were, it turned out, no less than twelve* Spandau *positions manned by paratroopers who meant to fight. Steadily and methodically B Company, under Major Beatson-Hird, who had commanded it in every action since D Day, dealt with each position in turn. Lieutenant Farmer and Sergeant Scanlon were afterwards decorated for the parts they played in this series of very gallant actions. At the sluice-gate on the riverside bund B Company linked up at last with the Argylls, who had cleared their section of the bund up to the sluice-gates...*

10 HLI made contact with 2 A&SH at 1200 hours. In summary:

> *In this bitter fight, in which they had met and worsted a complete parachute battalion which was fighting with all its*

**Clearing an enemy position built into a dyke.**

**The view inland from the dyke east towards Overkamp.**

*accustomed courage, the H.L.I. had lost three officers killed and four wounded, fourteen other ranks killed and seventy wounded. They had good reason to look back with pride on their Rhine crossing.*

Also crossing at 0200 hours, 2nd Argylls had considerable difficulty in getting their Buffaloes ashore due to sand and mud banks obstructing the proposed exits from the river. Their initial crossings, with D, B and A Companies in the first flight, were timed by their CO, Lieutenant Colonel Morgan, as taking twelve minutes rather than the two and a half where things had gone to plan.

See map on page 160

In the battalion plan, D Company was to have landed on the east side of the Hübsch inlet and to have gone straight for Hübsch and Lohr, where they would have been in touch with the HLI in Ree. Meanwhile, B and A Companies were to have landed west of the inlet and to have pushed north, astride the bund, towards Wayerhof, in preparation for an attack on Haffen from the west.

**Rosenhof Farm, the largest collection of buildings in Hübsch.**

In the event, five out of D Company's six Buffaloes, found it impossible to land at the eastern corner of the inlet as planned, so they climbed ashore on the west side. 'Thus D Company had a mile's march round the inlet before they could tackle Hübsch, so all hope of surprise was lost.' Worse than that, the Company had lost its commander and one platoon was missing for some time. Outside Hübsch they were engaged in some nasty close quarter fighting with *Fallschirmjäger*, who were positioned in strength along the reverse side of the bund and in the scrub to the southward. By first light, however, the Argyll's C Company had joined them, having crossed in the second flight of Buffaloes. D and C Companies together then cleared Hübsch, losing many men.

*There was considerable resistance centred on the houses at Hübsch, but after a sharp encounter this was cleared by D Company by first light. A patrol to the east along the bund, failed to contact 10 HLI as pre-arranged, and while on its way back, came under fire from* Spandaus *that had come to life after the artillery concentration lifted.*

Meanwhile, on the Argyll's left, B and A Companies who landed without casualties had pushed north without waiting for Hübsch to be cleared.

*After a stiff fight, A Company took Hoverhof, north-west of Haffen. B Company, farther east, beat off a two-company* Fallschirmjäger *counter-attack with the help of most effective defensive fire put down by the FOO, and took ninety prisoners. Thus, dawn found B and A Companies closely engaged with the enemy and separated by some two thousand five hundred yards from D and C in Hübsch. Battalion Headquarters was betwixt and between at Dornemardt.*

A and B Companies had marched north to reach their objectives around Wayerhof, known as Area X. In the process, they took some prisoners against patchy resistance, and encountering a few *schumines*. An attempt to capture Roperhof, however, failed and daylight revealed it as a strongpoint firmly held by the *Fallschirmjäger*. In carrying out this march, the Argylls had closed up to the right flank of 51st Highland Division in the form of 5/7 Gordons who were on the island formed by the old course of the Rhine. A physical link up was not, however, made until p.m. 26 March.

At 0615 hours, 227 Brigade's reserve battalion, 2 Gordons,

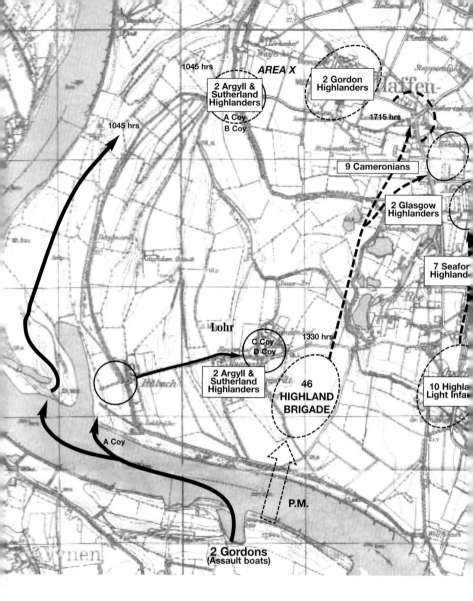

were ordered to send a company across the river, making this no less than three battalions of the same regiment taking part in the initial stages of the operation. As with all of the reserve battalions, the crossing was to be made in storm boats.

A Company who were ready to move, had been expecting to support 10 HLI but now found themselves cruising a mile down stream to land at Hübsch to join the Argylls. In doing so, they lost an officer and three other ranks killed and ten wounded to small arms fire from isolated enemy posts along the riverbank. B Company were ordered to cross but A Company's cruise in daylight, had alerted the enemy who mortared B Company very badly in their assembly area and with the loss of boats being a factor, temporarily abandoned the attempt. The presence of these isolated posts caused a significant delay in 15th Scottish Division's build-up during the morning of 24 March.

A Company joined the Argyll's D Company in advancing east, astride the road to Lohr at 0815 hours, while C Company (2 A&SH) went on to attack Riswickhof, a farm complex several hundred yards to the south. By the time the attack got going, the artillery check fire had been imposed, while air attacks prior to the airborne operation were launched. 1 Middlesex's medium machine guns, however, were available in quantity. The enemy put up significant resistance and it took the Scots

A British infantryman complete with his assault equipment.

infantry some time to break into the farms of Hangenshof and Riswickhof and it wasn't until 1330 hours that Lohr, five hundred yards further on, was clear. However, during the consolidation phase the Gordon's A Company lost their three remaining officers to a mortar barrage that struck while they were at an orders group.

Meanwhile, starting at 1030 hours, the remainder of 2 Gordons had crossed the river. Their historian wrote:

> ... the Battalion crossed to reinforce the Argyll. There were some minor troubles. The boat conveying the commanding officer and the adjutant ran out of petrol in mid-stream and was paddled until the sapper in charge produced a reserve tin.

Their task was to follow elements of the Argylls around the left flank to attack Haffen and secure the eastern part of Area X. This area in the centre of the 'Bend' formed a large area of houses, fields and orchards, and was a natural place for the Germans to defend. And so it proved, being firmly held by *18 Fallschirmjäger Regiment*. This large area was clearly too big for a single battalion to take and clear and, consequently, Divisional HQ needed to coordinate an attack on the eastern portion of the village by elements of 227 Highland Brigade. While this was coordinated, there would be another pause in operations.

**Divisional Reserve 46 Highland Brigade – Codeword WHIST**
Supported initially by the two DD squadrons and subsequently by the ordinary gun tanks, the highlanders of 46 Brigade, in a flexible plan, were responsible for expanding the bridgehead including clearing the woods overlooking Haldern. This brigade would also be responsible for forming the mobile striking force. First to cross, were 44 RTR and 7 Seaforth.

See map on page 146

Lieutenant Colonel Hopkinson, Commanding Officer of 44 RTR, whose unit had been on radio silence for the assembly and march down to the river, described his crossing operations, in 44 Lowland Brigade's area near Bislich:

> From then on we were 'on the air', as our far-bank reconnaissance and working parties, in two troops of Buffaloes, accompanied the assaulting infantry battalions across the Rhine. Their task was to prepare the two exits from the river, mark them, and exercise traffic control during the crossing.
>
> At last light all tanks had been pulled out of the leaguer on to the road and pointed in the right direction. Tea and rum was

**Sherman DDs on the east bank of the Rhine, shrouded with smoke.**

served at 0330 hours, and at 0400 the party moved off winding its way through the gun lines, some of which had to be silenced as we passed so as not to blow tank commanders' heads off. Slowly the column moved on down the hill through Xanten towards the 'inflation' area to the east of it.

On the other side of the river, the far bank reconnaissance parties had met with varying success. The right hand one was acting according to plan, but the left party had had a bit of trouble, and several casualties. It had been spandaued, mortared and shelled: however, it reported that it would be ready to receive the tanks on time.

By 0515 the unit was complete in the 'inflation' area, ready for the tricky operation of making the crossing. Luckily the enemy shelling was sporadic and not very accurate as far as we were concerned – not that it had to be, when all that was required was for one exhausted splinter to tear apart one's canvas. However, only two tanks were punctured and as dawn broke the unit started to move down to the water's edge. The crossing was made on a two-squadron front, A Squadron right, C Squadron left; R.H.Q. followed A Squadron, and B Squadron was held back ready to cross by either route. On the far bank both exits had by then been completed, and soon the river was full of tanks, looking rather like floating baths drifting downstream. Over half *of A Squadron was waterborne when the enemy started shelling the tanks. One tank was hit and sank like a stone; the crew luckily all abandoned ship and made the shore safely. R.H.Q. nipped in whilst the enemy was adjusting for range, and, except for a few splashes in midstream, had no trouble.*

*Meantime, C Squadron had got nine tanks waterborne, then the entrance started to collapse, so it was ordered to 'about face' the rest of the squadron and to follow on behind B Squadron, who were by now using the right-hand crossing. Tanks were now scrambling out of the exits in fine style, an alternative having been found for the left-hand exit. Reconnaissance officers had started to lead tanks away to the concentration area inland under the dyke. Here a certain amount of bogging took place in the thick clay belt on the far bank.*

*By now, 0815, the whole unit was across and concentrated, only half an hour above our estimate: contact had been established with an infantry battalion, 7th Seaforth, and we were ready to go.*

Having assembled on the flood plain behind 8 Royal Scots, the 44 RTR and Seaforth battle group awaited orders. By about 0900 hours the Divisional Commander was across the river and with his agreement, thirty minutes later, Brigadier Villers tasked A Company 7 Seaforth supported by the DD tanks to clear the bund and capture the area Sandenhof, (just north of Lohr) and if necessary assist 2 A&SH of 227 Brigade into Lohr. Forty-six prisoners from 1052 Grenadier Regiment (84th Division) were captured in the area Vissel–Treudekath and a further four prisoners from *21 Fallschirmjäger Regiment* at Wolffskath. This simple information confirmed the location of the German divisional boundary for the intelligence staff. The remainder of 7 Seaforth followed along the bund to Wolffskath. Here the battalion turned north, and, at 1300 hours, with some luck, infantrymen clinging to the Shermans of 44 RTR, began to pass through 10 HLI, with the object of seizing Mehr.

Lieutenant Colonel Hopkinson wrote:

**See map on page 173**

170

*Panzer* grenadiers and *Fallschirmjäger* evacuate a casualty of the fighting in a hand cart.

*Just after 1000 hours, we got definite orders that we and 7 Seaforth were to move north and link up the two bridgeheads. With B Squadron in the lead, we were soon in Vah on the right, where the bridge over the dyke was blown, and also in Wolffskath on the left near the Rhine bank. The enemy was still about and needed digging out of every building. He displayed his usual reluctance to surrender to tanks alone, so we kept infantry on our backs as long as possible in order to quicken things up. B Squadron now turned east, and joined up with 227 Brigade. C Squadron took up the chase and headed for Mehr. Apart from the bad going and a few snipers, no trouble was experienced in getting there. Meantime, A Squadron moved up on the left and got into Haffen, where it had a lot of fun with some good targets, while B Squadron, back from its 'swan' to 227th Brigade, stayed in the area of Overkamp to look after the tail end of the proceeding.*

The enemy had obviously intended to hold Mehr, as it was fortified and all roads and tracks were blocked and mined. In addition, the fire of enemy self-propelled guns covered all the roads and 'a brisk artillery duel was soon in progress'. Brigadier Villers, commander 46 Brigade, at this stage, however, called a halt to allow the rest of the brigade catch-up. To make use of the time, patrols were dispatched to recce bridges and get a better idea of the opposition's positions. The *Fallschirmjäger*, however, dispatched their own fighting patrols that followed the Scottish infantry, giving rise to alarm that they were launching a counter-attack. Whatever their intention, they were beaten off by C Squadron and elements of 7 Seaforth, supported by artillery. During these patrol actions the Seaforth were able to establish that the Germans were, predictably, holding the vital bridge across the old course of the Rhine in some strength.

46 Brigade's reorganisation included bringing up A Company 7 Seaforth from the Lohr area, which had just fallen to 2 A&SH. Once they had rejoined the battalion's main body, they followed up as battalion reserve into Mehr, which was reached at about 1530 hours but was not cleared by 1745 hours, yielding another sixty-eight prisoners. Opposition to the advance had come from *spandau* fire and some self-propelled guns. Mobility for the 44 RTR became a problem, when some bad going was encountered by the Shermans, with three tanks becoming bogged. The RTR were, none the less able to support the

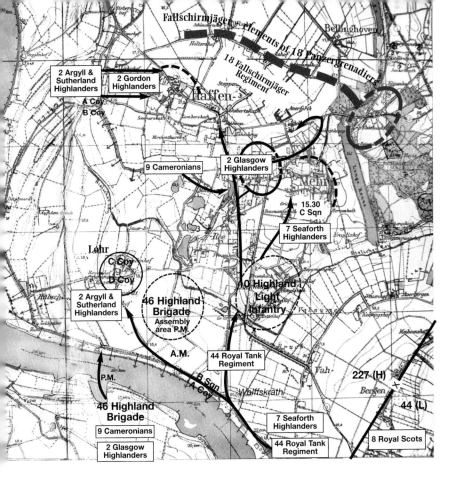

infantry's clearance of Mehr and drive off the enemy armour by sheer weight of numbers. Former RAF technician and Englishman, Ron James, found himself with the Seaforth Highlanders' B Company:

> My first battle was at Mehr. The village was a mess having been smashed up by our artillery and it was very difficult to spot the enemy in the confusion of blown down trees and rubble. Their game was to shoot as we advanced and then go into cover and try to escape and repeat the process over again. The paratroopers fought well but if they didn't have an officer or NCO with them they surrendered pretty quickly, especially when we got close or we had cut them off.

Up to this point, casualties in the battalion had been three officers and eighteen other ranks killed and wounded, and in 44 RTR one officer and five other ranks had been hit.

173

### The Attack on Haffen

Meanwhile, owing to the difficulty 227 Brigade had in clearing the river bend and reaching their objectives, the crossing of the remaining battalions of 46 Brigade had been badly delayed. 9 Cameronians began crossing by storm boat ferry at 1430 hours and was directed to join operations in the south eastern part of Haffen, which it will be recalled, was the largest area of houses, fields and orchards in the Bend area and, as was already apparent, was well defended by *18 Fallschirmjäger Regiment*. Divisional HQ coordinated a quick attack on Haffen by 2 Gordons of 227 Highland Brigade who were to clear the western portion of the village, while 9 Cameronians, supported by the Shermans of A Squadron 44 RTR, would approach from the south and southeast. Both battalions were conscious of the possibility of a blue and blue clash and as recalled by 2 Gordons, 'A certain amount of confusion was caused when some of our tanks were, erroneously, reported to be entering the village from the east'. This resulted in a 'check fire' being imposed on the artillery fire plan and the Scots attacking without the usual numbing deluge of shells. The difficulties, in mid-battle, of coordinating a quick attack from tactical headquarters, some of which were relying on man-pack sets, are easy to envisage.

See map on page 173

The Gordons' B and C Companies advanced through B Company 2 A&SH at 1715 hours across flat fields and orchards

**Medium guns in the Army Group Royal Artillery should have added weight to the fire plan for the attack on Haffen.**

into the western portion of the straggling village. Lieutenant Telfer was wounded in the fight to clear Haffen. Meanwhile, 9 Cameronian and A Squadron 44 RTR attacked Haffen from the south east. The squadron provided covering fire for the attack from the south and eventually the retreating enemy presented 'A Squadron with some excellent shooting'. By 1750 hours, the Cameronians had driven most of the *Fallschirmjäger* out and occupied the south eastern part of Haffen and the Gordons the western part. Despite seventy-one prisoners falling into the hands of the Gordons, the area was far from clear and indeed would not be considered a safe place until the following day.

See map on page 173

With Haffen and Mehr taken, the enemy was now holding the water obstacle of the Lange Renne and Hagener Meer, east and north east of Mehr, and 7 Seaforth was unable to advance further, not least because of the difficulties of armoured manoeuvre. Consequently, the Germans were able to hold an important bridge, which they eventually blew. The Seaforth went into positions holding the northern and northeastern outskirts of Mehr, which was now under enemy shellfire.

The Cameronians, even though detailed clearance of Haffen was still occupying their main attention, pushed several patrols north across the open ground, nearly as far as the line of the road Bruckshof–Holtershof where they were held up by *spandau* fire. During the afternoon's operations, 9 Cameronians suffered three officer and forty other rank casualties and took fifty prisoners.

2 Glasgow Highlanders eventually crossed the Rhine at 1645 hours and moved from the Forward Assembly Area to occupy a position between the Cameronians in Haffen and the Seaforth in Mehr, which was reached at 2300 hours, without opposition. This last move brought the majority of 15th Scottish into a solid position, although 227 Brigade, mainly due to delays in their crossing, had been halted short of Area 'Y' in the face of determined resistance by the *Fallschirmjäger*.

## 44 Lowland Brigade

We left this brigade on the Division's right flank, shortly after dawn, having occupied its initial objectives against slight opposition from the battered infantrymen of 84th Division. At 0700 hours, Brigadier Cumming-Bruce visited all his battalions in their initial positions and reported to General Barber that

The strain of battle is etched on the faces of these German soldiers.

'Progress was satisfactory' and that he was ordering his battalions forward to their final objectives.

This involved clearing hamlets and farms of the few members of 84th Division who were prepared to put up a fight and rounding up Germans who had gone to ground while the battle progressed. In the centre of the Brigade area, C and D Companies 6 KOSB cleared the straggling hamlet of Muhlenfeld by 1000 hours.

8 Royal Scots' next objectives were Vissel and Jockern, which the enemy still held. At 0945 hours, an attack was laid on to capture both these hamlets. B Company was directed on the Vissel, while D Company, commanded by Major J. N. Cadzow, attacked Jockern Incidental support was provided by B Squadron of 44 RTR, who at the crucial time was following 7 Seaforth (227 Highland Brigade) to the northwest and was able to engage targets in support of 8 RS. 'The two operations were entirely successful and numerous prisoners were taken in each of the hamlets.' However, coinciding with the arrival of the airborne armada overhead, there had been a noticeable slackening of resistance by the enemy infantry, who with the prospect of Allied paratroopers to their rear were increasingly reluctant to stand and fight. This, as we have seen, was in contrast with the experience of 227 Brigade, to the north west, who were facing the *Fallschirmjäger* all day.

Meanwhile, 6 RSF at the southern end of the Brigade's lodgement were to push forward from their initial objectives in Bislich/Marwick to Loh and thence patrol onward to the southern extension of the Dierfordterwald where they should make contact with elements of 17th US Airborne Division.

D Company on the right, were, according to Major Bokenham '... dug-in and alert, with some of the company relaxed a little to brew some tea'. This happy state of affairs was not, however, to last long. He continued:

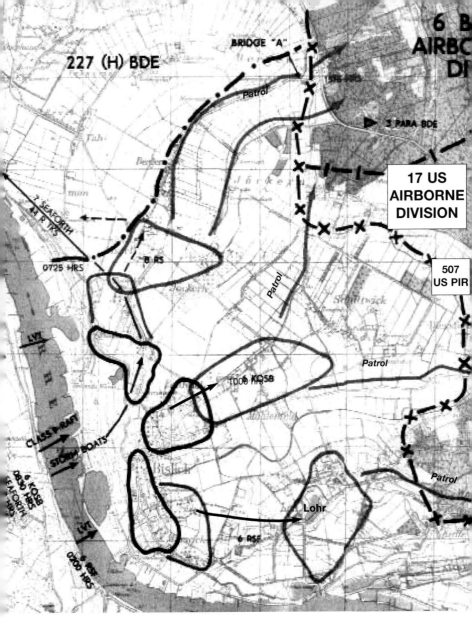

Orders were received to move further right to extend the bridgehead, and Captain Mann set off with Sergeant Curran's platoon to clear the route and captured a small harbour and several farmhouses, while a few men in the company remained to hold a firm base. Using fire and movement to perfection, Captain Mann's men routed a spandau post on the way to their *objective, succeeded in clearing the target without loss, and took another fifty-three prisoners. The rest of the company joined them and dug in on its final objective. Patrols went out and a further nineteen prisoners were gathered without loss. The night was spent safely in this position, but there was some unpleasantness from fire on our own side of the Rhine at mines in the river, as well as from a machine-gunning dive attack by an enemy jet aircraft.*

As indicated by Major Bokenham's account, patrols had been dispatched by all three of 44 Brigade's battalions across a mile or more of open ground to the Diesrfordterwald. The landing of the Airborne Corps had completed the total disruption of the 84th Divisions defence and the patrols were able to reach the wood. 6 KOSB, being the nearest, contacted 507 Parachute Infantry Regiment in the village of Diesrfordter at 1400 hours and further south, 6 RSF joined the Americans at 1510. Yellow celanese triangles were carried by all ranks of the assault brigades and contact frequencies were allocated to reduce the likelihood of 'blue on blue' contact. 8 RS reached 6th British Airborne Division near Bergen at 1515, having secured Bridge A *en route*. The important link up had occurred. This would enable the Airborne troops to concentrate on facing east across the River Issel and for 15th Scottish Division to place their main effort further north with the aim of extending the bridgehead and closing up to the Issel.

## XII Corps Evening Situation Report

The Corps had every right to be pleased with its achievements against an enemy that had already proved to be resolute in the defence of his Fatherland during the battles in the Reichswald, Cleve, Goch, etc. during Operations VERITABLE and BLOCKBUSTER. XII Corps summed up the enemy position at the end of D Day in the following words:

*There were no surprises in the enemy layout opposing us. As expected 84 Inf Div proved to be in control from the LIPPE river to the area of VISSEL with: from left to right the WESEL Garrison, 1052 GR, 1062 (Mt) Regt and 1051 GR. Moreover, if the PoW figures are to be trusted, the division seems to be well in the running for a second destruction within a period of six weeks. Our own total of PoWs must be well over a thousand while the, airborne forces claim 3,504 and a high proportion of both totals must come from the luckless 84 Inf Div. Incidentally, to round off what must have been a black day for the division, its HQ was bombed this morning.*

*By comparison, 7 Para Div, whose right extends on to our left-hand neighbour's front (30 Corps), has not fared too badly. Both 19 and 21 Para Regts have been identified, but so far 20 Para Regt does not appear to have been involved.*

While 84th Division may have had an extremely 'black day' and virtually ceased to exist, *15th Panzergrenadier Division* was attempting to fill the vacuum and was still full of fight.

### German Counter-Attack

As night fell on 24 March, the pace of operations slackened and soldiers who had only snatched moments of sleep in the previous forty-eight hours got what rest they could. Meanwhile, with all their offensive efforts in daylight frustrated by British

See map on page 173

artillery fire, the *Fallschirmjäger*, now reinforced by *15th Panzer Grenadiers*, were planning to counter-attack the Scots.

Initial enemy operations were focused in the east and south eastern sectors of 7 Seaforth positions, but were driven off by accurate shooting of C Squadron 44 RTR and F Battery 4th Royal Horse Artillery. Colonel Hopkinson of 44 RTR had just received orders to regroup his squadrons, for the following day's operations, when an altogether more serious enemy attack began.

A *panzergrenadier* armed with a *panzerfaust*.

*Accordingly A and C Squadrons were pulled back. Just as we were leaving 46 Brigade staked a claim for one squadron to stay right in support of them, so B Squadron moved up behind Mehr. The enemy put in a fairly fierce counter-attack as we left, and employed more artillery on it than at any other time during the battle.*

Then at midnight, this 'considerable

179

counter-attack' developed from the northeast, and parties of enemy succeeded in infiltrating into 7 Seaforth's positions, forcing C Company to withdraw. Between 0300 and 0330 hours, 'after making the awkward decision to use medium artillery' close to positions defensive artillery fire was called for in the area previously occupied by the company, in the south eastern corner of Mehr, and medium guns of the A.G.R.A. engaged the wooded areas to the east and north-east of the town. The enemy succeeded in infiltrating to Merrbruch, where earlier in the evening another four Shermans of C Squadron 44 RTR had become bogged, while moving to a night leaguer. The crews deployed their pintel mounted Browning machine guns in the ground role. Despite their fire one of the stranded tanks was knocked out by a *Panzerfaust*, and the remaining three had to be set on fire by their crews, since, for security reasons, the risk of DD tanks falling into enemy hands could not be accepted. Colonel Hopkinson noted that the B Squadron and C Squadron's crews 'had a pretty hectic night, in particular the bogged crews who were overrun by an enemy infantry company and spent the rest of the night fighting on their feet ...'.

Brigadier Villiers ordered 7 Seaforth to hold its positions and 2 Glasgow Highlanders were warned to assist if required. Between 0430 hours and 0630 hours 25 March, the right of the Glasgow Highlanders' positions was also attacked and C Company was temporarily pinned down in its trenches, finally making a successful withdrawal covered by smoke.

According to the British Army of the Rhine's historian, writing in 1947:

> The position in 7 Seaforth's sector was stabilised by 0500 hours, the enemy withdrawing slowly, he was finally ejected from the town by 0700 hours, and companies were able to reoccupy their former positions. One officer and twenty-one other ranks of 7 Seaforth had become casualties, and the enemy lost over thirty prisoners and a number of dead and wounded.

Most of the Seaforth taken prisoner by the *Fallschirmjäger* escaped during the subsequent chaotic days. The counter-attack had been held but was to impose a delay on opening the next phase of the battle.

# CHAPTER 7

# Operation VARSITY

EVEN THOUGH the British and Canadian element of the airborne assault, Operation VARSITY, will be covered in a separate *Battleground* volume, it was an important component of the overarching operation to cross the Rhine, Operation PLUNDER VARSITY cannot, therefore, be entirely put to one side. Consequently, this chapter is an outline only of the main action.

As the Scottish infantry and commandos fought their way east of the Rhine, XVIII US Airborne Corps prepared to leave its transit camps on the morning of 24 March 1945. The two component divisions were in separate countries, 6th British Airborne Division was back in southern England while 17th US were based around Paris.

On a bright and clear morning, the aircraft bearing 6th Airborne Division took off from eleven air bases around East Anglia. First away, from 0700 hours, were the two parachute brigades, whose Dakota aircraft led the stream of aircraft to the Rhine. Meanwhile, the Airlanding Brigade moved to their three departure airfields where their heavily laden gliders waited on the runways.

The Dakota parachute aircraft, were followed by the Stirling, Halifax and Dakota tug aircraft of Number 38 and 46 Groups, with the gliders of the Glider Pilot Regiment bearing 6 Airlanding Brigade. They flew south and crossed the coast near Hastings but, however, they had the usual towing problems. For instance, 12 Devons, being

**General Lewis Bereton Commander of the First Allied Air Army.**

towed by Stirling tugs, lost five gliders and some important men and equipment.

The British aircraft flew to a point south of Brussels, where they met the stream of aircraft carrying 17th US Airborne Division. The total number of aircraft was in excess of 1,500 parachute aircraft and 1,300 tug/glider combinations, bearing nearly 17,000 men, 600 tons of ammunition and 800 vehicles and guns.

The two streams of XVIII US Airborne Corps' aircraft headed east towards the Rhine. Lieutenant Colonel Hewson of 8 Para recalled that:

*The flight was uneventful. It was a sunny clear day, and occasionally during the flight, I looked through the door and saw the most impressive stream of aircraft. Over the Continent, we passed under the glider stream, which would be released half-an-hour after the parachutists.*

**Gliderborne infantry training prior to the operation.**

**Enemy Forces**

In his post war interrogation, Major General Fiebig who commanded *84th Volksgrenadier Division*:

> ... claimed that the Germans were not unaware of our preparations for an airborne operation in support of the Rhine crossings and appreciated that no fewer than four allied airborne divisions were available, although he confessed he had been badly surprised by the sudden advent of two complete divisions in this particular area, and throughout the interrogation reiterated the shattering effect of such immensely superior forces on his already badly depleted troops, which did not number more than 4,000 in all.

> General Fiebig had no exact advance information about landing and dropping zones, or times, although he had fully appreciated the likelihood of a landing somewhere in his area. He rather expected the landing farther from the Rhine, in the area east of the River Issel and thought it would take place either at dusk before the land assault or else simultaneously with it.

**The Airborne Plan**

General Sir Miles Dempsey considered it 'absolutely essential to have airborne assistance in crossing the Rhine'. The airborne mission was to be twofold:

*(1) Seize the commanding ground from which artillery fire controlled the whole area.*

*(2) Block possible arrival of enemy reinforcements ...*
According to Montgomery, it was decided to drop XVIII Airborne Corps east of the Rhine after 21st Army Group's main assault for:

> Two main reasons ... daylight was desirable for the employment of airborne troops and, secondly, it would be impossible to make full use of our artillery for the ground assault if airborne troops were dropped in the target area before we had crossed the river.

**General Ridgeway who had to execute Dempsey's Plan.**

The risks of dropping on top of the enemy were considerable, as the airborne would be at their most vulnerable when landing but the two divisions of the Corps were planned to land well concentrated, after a heavy bombardment.

## Corps Plan

Ridgeway's XVIII US Airborne Corps was to land, with a P Hour of 1000 hours on 24 March, three to six miles east of the Rhine, in order to dislocate the enemy defences, seize vital

ground, and take the Issel bridges, which were necessary for the breakout onto the North German Plain. The bridges once captured, were to be held but prepared for demolition in case they should fall into the hands of the German *XLVII Panzer Corps*, who would themselves need the bridges for their counter-attack against XII Corps bridgehead.

The entire Corps would be flown in a single lift and would be dropped on its objectives, within range of medium artillery west of the Rhine. It was planned that 15th Scottish Division and US infantry would link-up with the airborne troops on the first day of the battle.

**Shoulder flash of XVIII US Airborne Corps HQ.**

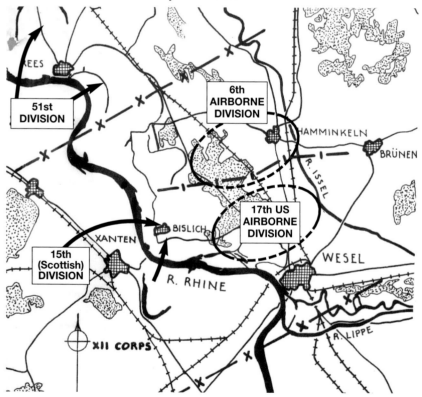

## 6th Airborne Division's Plan

Major General Bols's plan was to drop and land in front of XII Corps, with the tasks of seizing the wooded high ground of the Dierfordterwald, the large village of Hamminkeln and three bridges over the River Issel. Linking up with 17th US Airborne Division and forming a defensive northern flank were also important considerations.

**The Pegasus badge, symbol of British Airborne Forces.**

In detail, 3 Parachute Brigade was to lead the operation by dropping on DZ A at the north west corner of the Dierfordterwald, then to clear the forest, overlooking XII Corps' routes. Meanwhile, on DZ B to the north of Hamminkeln, 5 Parachute Brigade would drop, clear and secure the area. While patrolling westwards, the Brigade was to hold the area to the east of the railway line.

The Airlanding Brigade, coming in after the two parachute brigades was to land in company groups as close as possible to their objectives. 2 Ox and Bucks LI and 1 RUR were to mount *coups de main* on the Issel bridges. Intelligence, however, revealed that there were numerous flak positions in the area of their LZs. Following 6th Airlanding Brigade, Divisional HQ and the Airborne Division's artillery group would land by glider on LZ P.

A divisional reserve was to be provided by eight Locust tanks from the Armoured Recce Regiment. They were to fly into LZ P, with one 7-ton tank per Hamilcar glider, along with guns of the Anti-Tank Regiment, who would be deployed, as needed, to blunt German counter-attacks.

## The Parachute Drop – 3 Para Brigade

Seven minutes early, the first Dakota aircraft carrying Brigadier James Hill's 3 Parachute Brigade was flying in over the Rhine. 'Enemy anti-aircraft fire was moderate when the leading aircraft arrived, but became more intense for successive waves, as the enemy began to recover from the anti-flak bombardment, and the gun positions had not yet been overrun.'

Approaching DZ A, Colonel Hewson recalled the final minutes of the flight:

*At 0946 hours, we were given the order 'Five minutes to go'.*
*I remember feeling very apprehensive about this as according to*

**Allied paratroopers drop east of the Rhine.**

*the time given this would mean dropping on the wrong side of the RHINE. However, at 0951 hours we crossed the RHINE with the usual sinking feeling of impending 'baling out'. I remember looking forward from the door and seeing the fog of battle on the ground, the aftermath of the terrific pounding from our massed artillery. Red light–green light–out–parachute open–ground fairly hard–sigh of relief!*

The drop was well concentrated with only a few sticks going astray.

Once on the ground, the battalions set about completing their initial tasks. 8 Para secured the DZ and was then to hold the northern part of the Dierfordterwald; 9 Para set out to seize the south eastern part of the wood including the Schnappenburg feature, while 1 Canadian Para advanced through the trees to occupy the central area of the forest.

Dropping on top of the enemy meant that the paratroopers were immediately embroiled in some serious close quarter fighting. Casualties on the DZ were to be expected but were heavy. The CO of 1 Canadian Para was killed while hung up in a tree and Corporal Topham, from the same battalion, received a VC for his part in clearing casualties from the DZ under fire. Once off the DZ, the three parachute battalions moved to occupy positions in the Dierfordterwald, fighting small but sharp

Corporal Topham VC.

engagements with groups of enemy in the woods and around gun positions. Casualties continued to be significant but by early afternoon the Brigade's objectives were secure.

### 5 Para Brigade

Arriving on DZ B, fifteen minutes behind the leading elements, Brigadier Poett's 5 Para Brigade was met by increasing enemy flak. Having dropped their paratroopers, the Dakotas turned north and in doing so, they caught even heavier fire. Seventy aircraft were hit and damaged; ten being shot down, with a further seven coming down before reaching their bases.

Brigade HQ jumped at 1010, followed by 13, 12 and 7 Para. The Brigade's signallers had jumped with the new more powerful rear link No. 52 sets in their kit bags. The communications lessons of Arnhem had been learned and opening radio frequencies had been 'netted by pre-checked crystal wave meters, and the dials locked and sealed before loading'. New radios were complemented by better liaison between Second Army and XVIII Airborne Corps and the parachute elements of

**Brigadier James Hill visiting the Canadian Para battalion during VARSITY.**

the Artillery Forward Observation Unit (FOU) were soon speaking to FOU liaison officers west of the Rhine.

About an hour after the drop, 5 Para Brigade's three battalions were sufficiently complete in their RVs to be able to report that they were ready to start on the second phase of the plan: the securing and consolidating of the brigade objectives. 5 Para Brigade was to protect the northern front of the Corps area. 7 Para were to secure the DZ and cover the northeasterly approach into the divisional area until 15th Scottish Division arrived. 12 and 13 Para were to both hold key counter-attack routes into the divisional area.

Having suffered heavier casualties during their drop and in the early stages of the battle, the paratroopers, in more exposed positions, were subjected to sharp counter-attacks but they held their ground.

### Later Action

Having taken and secured their objectives between midday and 1300 hours, the plan for the two parachute brigades was to dominate the ground with aggressive patrols, to cover gaps and to identify enemy attempting to advance or infiltrating through their part of the Divisional area.

In some places, they rounded up stray Germans, while in others, they were ambushing and being ambushed or fighting-off organised groups of up to platoon strength. Meanwhile, the brigades' support elements and supplies were dropped in, suffering casualties both in the air and on the ground.

**Paratroops hastily dug in before the counter-attacks began.**

The link up with the leading elements of 15th Scottish Division was made at 1515 hours on 24 March, at a small bridge to the west of the Dierfordterwald Bridge A. As already recorded, first to reach the 3 Para Brigade was 8 Royal Scots, with patrols from 6 Kings Own Scottish Borderers contacting 9 Para a little further south. Radio contact had also been established to manage the approach of two friendly forces during the height of a battle. At 1545 hours, Commander 44 Infantry Brigade and the Commanding Officer of 8 Royal Scots arrived at HQ 3 Para Brigade and 'were given a rousing reception by the parachutists'.

## 6 Air Landing Brigade

Following the two parachute brigades was the Airlanding Brigade, aboard 196 Horsa gliders. The task given to them was to seize three crossings of the River Issel, for both offensive and defensive purposes, and to take important road junctions and villages. Ultimately, the Airlanding Brigade was to hold approaches into the divisional area from the east against armoured counter-attacks that could be expected two hours after landing.

With the German anti-aircraft gunners having recovered from the bombardment, they switched their fire from the Dakotas to the incoming gliders. The gliders cast off from their tugs at 2,500 feet, at 1015 hours were sweeping down towards their LZs. The Airlanding Brigade suffered cruelly from flak and other ground fire, which they had been briefed would be well suppressed. Some German prisoners taken during VARSITY, later claimed they knew the gliders were coming and that in fact they were late.

Enemy fire was only one of the problems facing the glider pilots. Ground obscuration was another problem, as Harry Clark recalled:

*As we crossed over the Rhine at an altitude of some 5000 feet, the river appeared as a narrow twisting silvery ribbon. The Horsa cast off from its tug aircraft about two miles over the enemy side of the river. We could see a dense wall of smoke drifting across the battlefield from the direction of Wesel and one of the pilots shouted out that the LZ was obscured by the haze and smoke. Anti-aircraft fire began to intensify as we rapidly lost altitude. We plunged into the smoke. Most of the men in the*

189

*Horsa sat silently in their seats, waiting for the certain impact of the crash landing that would shortly occur. Our glider hit the ground at approx 90mph losing the wheels on impact. Pieces of wings were torn off as we went through a series of ditches and hedges. We came to a halt and swiftly removed ourselves from the battered wreckage.*

The Brigade's leading gliders were heading for *coup de main* attacks on three bridges across the Issel. The bridge carrying the Hamminkeln road east was to be captured by 1 RUR and a pair of bridges, further north, were to be seized by 2 Ox & Bucks LI. (the same).

## The Landing Zone

The landings on LZs U and O were chaotic, as not only was the brigade landing through thick haze and smoke but also in the presence of enemy anti-aircraft guns. To make matters worse, as landings began *Kampfgruppe Krafft*, an armoured battle group in the anti-airborne role was approaching the LZs. Their tactical doctrine was to drive into the teeth of an airborne landing, before the force could form up.

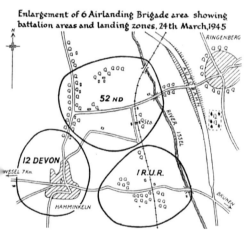

Enlargement of 6 Airlanding Brigade area showing battalion areas and landing zones, 24th March,1945

In the confusion about half of B Company of the 12 Devons, as noted by Lieutenant Allinson, 'advanced in what we thought to be the right direction but after finding our position from a civilian, we returned to our original area and advanced on Hamminkeln'. Small, disconnected actions were taking place all over the battlefield preventing men from concentrating on their objectives. Brigadier Bellamy wrote that '... ground opposition was stronger than anticipated, every farmhouse was a strong point and there was a considerable number of enemy SP guns and half tracks milling around the Brigade area'. In many cases only a small fraction of men planed were able to attack their targets but as Brigadier Bellamy continued:

*... sufficient troops of each battalion were landed in the correct*

190

**A wrecked Horsa which brought in the Devons. Behind is Hamminkeln Church.**

*places, and most important of all, a percentage of the* coup-de-main *parties landed by the bridges. All-important objectives were either in our hands or neutralised and ready for plucking by 1130 hours.*

1 RUR reported that they were, in position southeast of Hamminkeln, and the Ox and Bucks were reporting that although they were at their objective, they numbered only two hundred men and were under mounting pressure. However, 12 Devon's clearance of the village of Hamminkeln would take longer.

## Hamminkeln

Hamminkeln is a large village in the centre of the divisional area, which, if held by the enemy, could dominate a large area of ground and deny an important road hub. Failure to capture it promptly would mean a protracted battle and require numerous troops to overcome. This made Hamminkeln the Brigade's most important objective but the Devons were scattered and it took Lieutenant Colonel Gleadell some time to collect enough men to establish a thin cordon around Hamminkeln and to mount an attack. Colonel Gleadell recalled:

*... I myself joined up with a platoon of D Company and we concentrated about the road junction north of the village and, after encountering some resistance, reached the northern edge of Hamminkeln.*

Corporal Anderson's version of these events is, however, more revealing:

> By the time we were ready to move, more men had joined us, and we now mustered nearly fifty, to capture the town of Hamminkeln ... An undertaking for which our planners had allocated five hundred men ...
>
> The Germans had snipers covering almost every section of the elevated roadway. However, there were houses that might offer cover at intervals of about two hundred yards or so along the road. So the Colonel told us to leap-frog from one to another, spacing ourselves from five to ten yards apart, running like hares and only regrouping when we arrived at the outskirts of the town.

Reaching the first house, the Devons kicked the doors in 'hoping to God the Jerries have only got small arms and that there aren't any tanks or artillery to shell the houses'. Colonel Gleadell commented that 'The capture of Hamminkeln was to begin at 1135 hours. The companies duly assaulted the village and the objective was taken by midday.'

The task was not, however, as easy as it sounds. Under fire from unseen riflemen in the houses of Hamminkeln, fitness counted. Corporal Anderson dived through a gap in a hedge, wriggled on his stomach to the door and moved quickly inside. Having cleared the house they were preparing for their next dash:

> The colonel was already knocking out the window frame on the opposite side of the house. Through the window he climbed and was off on the next lap of his mad journey. The batman and I followed. Behind me I could hear footsteps and hoped that the rest of the platoon were still coming on, but there was no time even to turn my head to see as it was a good two hundred yards, probably more, to the next house ... the German snipers had realized that ...their best opportunity was to concentrate their fire about ten yards from the house. The colonel made it safely, but his batman went down about ten yards from safety.

The battle became confused and the house clearing drills learned in the abandoned villages of Salisbury Plain, came into play. Corporal Anderson recounted:

> The colonel advanced to the first doorway, while my men and I, with our backs to the wall on the other side of the road, covered

*every doorway and window on his side. When he was safely in position, it was our turn to advance, while he covered us. So, doorway by doorway, house by house, we crept forward.*

*Suddenly, machine-gun fire spurted from an upstairs window just ahead. I burst open the front door of the next house on our side, closely followed by two men. They ran upstairs and I began firing at the house from which the firing had come... Keeping close to the wall, the Colonel inched along with his back to the wall. When they arrived at the manned house, they tossed grenades through the front door... As soon as the grenades had exploded, the three men ran into the house. I heard a rattle of gunfire from inside and then the men emerged, covered with dust but unhurt ...*

**Corporal Dudley Anderson.**

Presently Anderson and the Devons reached the main square of Hamminkeln, which was dominated by a large building over which a swastika was flying that proved to be the local anti-aircraft headquarters. He was ordered by the Colonel to

**A high priority was placed on radio communications from the Rhine crossing.**

take his 'section and clear it while I carry on through the town'. With the Devons fanning out around the town, the last resistance was quickly mopped up, which 'was vigorously carried out in anticipation of the expected counter-attack and to eliminate the remaining flak positions'.

## Conclusion

As dusk fell on 24 March, despite 6th Airborne's patrols combing the woods, farms and villages the enemy, many of whom had been lying-up until dark, became more active, either with aggressive intent or simply trying to exfiltrate to their own lines under the cover of darkness.

With paratroopers and glider infantry dropping behind them, the already weakened 84th Division dissolved before 15th Scottish Division. Though costly in terms of casualties, the drop had dislocated the enemy and secured the crossings of the Issel, which almost certainly would have been firmly held by *XLVII Panzer Korps* by the time XII Corps arrived.

## Chapter Eight

# The Capture of Rees

WE LEFT XXX CORPS' Operation TURNSCREW in Chapter 4, with 51st Highland Division firmly ashore on the east bank of the Rhine, and all three of its brigades across the river. 154 Brigade on the left flank had faced some stiff opposition from the *Fallschirmjäger* in Esserden and had been forced to withdraw from Speldrop, by a vigorous and well coordinated German counter-attack. Meanwhile, 153 Brigade had crossed the Rhine astride Rees to form a bridgehead and 1 Gordons were attacking the outskirts of Rees from the west. With the crossing going well, the divisional reserve, 152 Brigade, had assembled two battalions on the far bank of the Rhine. 2 Seaforth had successfully advanced across some difficult country to seal off Rees from the north by establishing themselves in a factory complex. However, the Seaforth were in an exposed position, as 5 Cameronian were unable to cross the Millinger Meer to come

**The town of Rees viewed from the west bank at the time of the attack.**

into the line on their left. The divisional reserve consisted of a single battalion of 152 Brigade; 5 Seaforth, who would be ferried across the Rhine during the course of the morning.

Overall, 51st Highland Division's situation was favourable despite growing enemy reaction in the form of determined counter-attacks that included armour from *15th Panzer Grenadiers*. However, the two DD squadrons of the Sherwood Rangers were now ready for action and the Highland Light Infantry of Canada (HLI of C) were crossing and would support 154 Brigade in Speldrop and Bienen.

The picture was not entirely rosy, as the inspirational and popular divisional commander, Major General Rennie, had been killed by mortar fire. This increased the pressure on the brigade commanders, as for some time they came more immediately under XXX Corps' command and received the personal attention of General Horrocks. It was, of course, impractical to extricate a brigade commander in mid battle. However, Brigadier Oliver temporarily took over before an Argyll officer known to the division, Major General MacMillan, (nicknamed 'Babe') took command of this most 'tribal and temperamental of British divisions'. The new commander arrived from the 49th Division on the morning of 25 March.

### The Defence of Rees
The *II Fallschirmjägerkorps* had fully appreciated that by holding Rees they could potentially dominate the Rhine bridging sites either side of the town. While they would probably be unable to prevent an assault crossing, they could prevent or badly delay the consolidation and build up of Allied forces on the eastern bank, making them extremely vulnerable to counter-attack by *XVII Panzerkorps*. Therefore, Rees was to be held by *12 Fallschirmjäger Battalion* under *Hauptmann* Hubner, reinforced by a

**Major General 'Babe' MacMillan.**

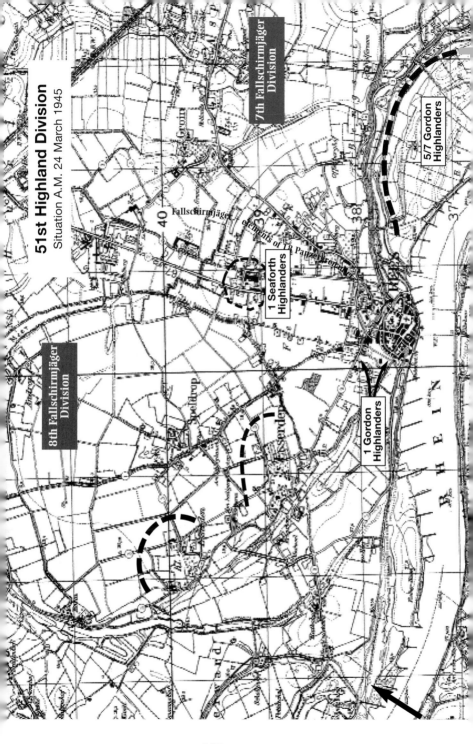

**51st Highland Division**
Situation A.M. 24 March 1945

7th Fallschirmjäger Division

8th Fallschirmjäger Division

5/7 Gordon Highlanders

1 Seaforth Highlanders

1 Gordon Highlanders

Fallschirmjäger elements of 18 Panzergrenadier

Speldrop

R H E I N

197

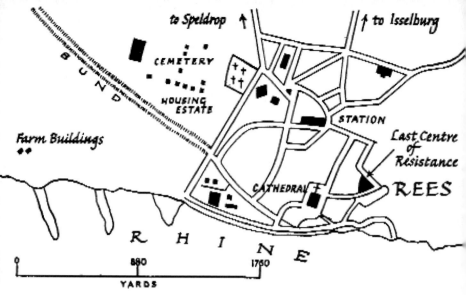

'battalion' of *Volkssturm* and supported by some of the *Fallschirmjäger*'s self-propelled artillery. These were mainly improvised equipment made up from tank or other AFV hulls and the guns from towed artillery pieces. A German civilian reports that a *Fallschirmjäger* company commander told him that his command, at just fifty men, was the strongest company in the battalion.

*Hauptmann* Hubner's tactics were similar to those that the Wesel Garrison had intended to use but in their case, they had been negated by the Allied bomber strikes. Hubner's plan was based on the development of a number of well-prepared strongpoints at key locations within the town. These companies or more likely platoon strength positions, were sited to block likely Allied approaches and included substantial buildings that dominated these routes and were suitable for use as artillery or mortar observation posts.

Selected buildings put into a state of defence, invariably had a good strong cellar in which the defenders could shelter from the expected Allied artillery bombardment. To make an effective strongpoint a building would also have to have a good field of fire, covering the likely enemy assault routes and dominate surrounding houses. The buildings would be strengthened; potential entrances barricaded and concealed loopholes made in the walls and roofs. Inside, old-fashioned murder holes were cut to enable the defenders to drop grenades on attackers breaking in below. Finally, routes for the defenders to redeploy were

Labels on image: Cemetery, B Coy, C Coy, The north-south road, Mill Tower, Square, Cathedral, Home Bank

**A composite air photograph of Rees before the battle.**

created by 'mouse holing' from room to room and house to house and covered escape routes planned. This would enable the defenders to withdraw to their next prepared position, having inflicted the maximum casualties and delay on the attackers.

Supplementing the strongpoints, which were principally held by *Volkssturm* under the eye of *Fallschirmjäger* officers and NCOs, would be patrols of veteran soldiers who were to provide a defensive perimeter to identify the routes that the Allies were actually taking, cover flanks and gaps between the strongpoints. These patrols were to play an essential part in inflicting attrition on the Scots and delaying them by forcing time-consuming clearance of buildings that were not in fact prepared for defence. An important task of the patrols was to hunt down and destroy with *Panzershrecks* or *Panzerfausts*, their priority target, British flame-throwing tanks – Crocodiles or the smaller carrier version the Wasp.

In summary capturing a medium sized town that the enemy had been afforded time to prepare for defence was going to be a protracted affair.

## The Clearance of Rees

By 0800 hours B Company 1 Gordon Highlanders reached their first objective in the northwest corner of Rees; a cemetery, from where they took up a defensive position to protect C Company's attack into the centre of the town. This company had just broken through the *Fallschirmjäger*'s perimeter defences and was fighting in the outskirts of the town.

C Company reported slow but steady progress in the difficult task of clearing a determined enemy from well-concealed positions, made worse by Rees's state of ruin and chaos. Houses were shattered, streets blocked by shell craters and rubble, which the *Fallschirmjäger* were using to good advantage to supplement the defended buildings. The Gordons were completely unaware of the extent of preparations made by the enemy.

During the fighting, it is recorded that Private Blackman narrowly escaped being killed, when he was shot at by a German armed with *panzerfausts*, as he was observing from a window of a partly ruined house. Outraged, he set out on a personal vendetta:

> ... *which was to continue to the end of the war, in search of the German who had shot at him, the PIAT was the British equivalent of the Panzerfaust and by this stage of the war had earned the reputation of being more dangerous to the firer than the target. Despite this Blackman began to fire his PIAT at any Germans he saw, this was to have a very salutary effect on the German resistance in his immediate vicinity.*

Private Blackman was awarded the Distinguished Conduct Medal for his determined actions during the clearance of Rees.

C Company fought through to their objective in the town to

**Lightly armed and equipped youthful defenders of the Reich prepare to repel invaders.**

a line west of the square by 1000 hours. While they had been fighting to clear the houses and buildings, D Company, having been relieved of rear area security by A Company, had advanced eastwards along the riverbank and without encountering enemy positions, was able to link up with C Company in the

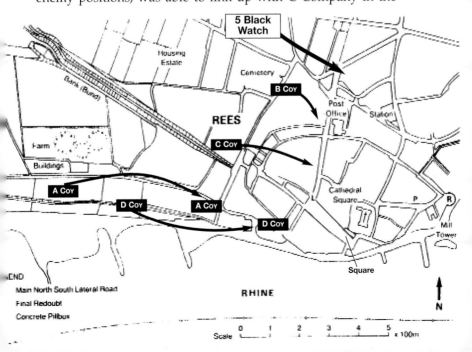

**The North-South Road today from the area of the post office looking south to the river.**

town. Unfortunately, in doing so, one of the platoon commanders of D Company, 'Lieutenant Rodger and his platoon sergeant, Sergeant Mathews, had been killed by a shell whilst sheltering in a German trench on the riverbank. This was a particularly cruel double blow to the Company as Sergeant Mathews was one of only a few Senior NCOs who were experienced enough to act as a platoon commander'.

A Company still following up behind the advance, promptly

**The North-South Road looking north to the Post Office.**

relieved D Company of holding the newly captured area at 1030 hours and set about dominating this outskirt of Rees and kept the streets clear of enemy displaced from the central area. With the ground behind them secured by A Company, D Company continued its advance along the riverbank and managed to clear as far as the main town square.

Prisoners being brought west along the bund to Colonel Grant-Peterkin's Headquarters, were questioned by the intelligence officer who confirmed that the enemy they were facing were a battalion from 8th *Fallschirmjäger* Division and a *Landschutzen* battalion. With similar reports from 5/7 Gordons, this confirmed that 153 Brigade had landed astride the boundary between 7th and 8th *Fallschirmjäger* Divisions.

While A and D Companies dominated the southern part of Rees, C Company turned north and cleared the intervening streets, linking up with B Company. All three of the forward companies, B, C and D, now held a four hundred yard linked frontage within the town. By 1220 hours, the town was clear of enemy to within fifty yards of the main north-south road that bisected the town. The Commanding Officer recorded in his post operational report that:

**Fallschirmjäger had to be cleared from strongly constructed buildings and piles of rubble.**

*The Germans ... concentrated in and fought from the key buildings, and then from the ground floors; only the odd* Spandau *and snipers were up a storey or two. Booby traps were not met with in any large numbers; mines were, however, lain in and around all their demolitions, key road junctions and in some gardens, but the latter were usually marked.*

With his battalion well balanced, Colonel Grant-Peterkin ordered

A Company to prepare to move up and occupy the rubble along the western edge of the main north-south road. However, during a preliminary recce, Major Rare came under fire from enemy held houses on the east side of the road that dominated the area. Consequently, the CO decided to leave A Company in its present position. The battalion had now been in action for a considerable time and the Colonel realised that reorganisation and re-supply was needed.

*At 1600 hours, however, Brigadier Sinclair had reviewed the situation and ordered that the clearing of Rees was:*

*"... to continue without pause, throughout the night if the operation should take so long and that, at all costs it must be cleared by first light on the 25th."*

The 5 Black Watch who had been one of the initial assault battalions, was now in reserve and would assist by clearing the town to the north of the station road and carry out a company attack on the railway station itself at 2300 hours. The CO, Colonel Bradford, however, seeing how exhausted his men where, asked if the operation could be postponed until an hour before first light, as a night clearing operation through the rubble of Rees seemed impossible. His men had, after all, now been awake for over twenty-four hours and needed rest. Such a delay could not be sanctioned, as the Corps Commander, General Horrocks, wanted Rees cleared 'as a matter of highest priority'. Until this was achieved, the enemy artillery observation posts concealed within the town could prevent, or at least severely hinder, the construction of the bridges that would allow armour and other heavy equipment to cross the Rhine, prevent the battle developing as planned and leave the bridgehead vulnerable to counter-attack. (*See map opposite.*)

The unusual interference in battalion level operations by the Corps Commander was the result of General Rennie's death. With the Highland Division's brigades locked in combat, and with only one division in action, it was an easy decision for the Corps Commander, with his own tactical HQ, to effectively take over command of the division. Major Lindsay recalled seeing the Corps Commander with his CO and Brigadier Oliver, who was nominally commanding the division but in reality fighting the battle for Rees, 'planning the coming night's operations ...'

The 5 Black Watch attack began shortly after dark and, as described by the regimental historian:

Engineer Operations in Support of PLUNDER

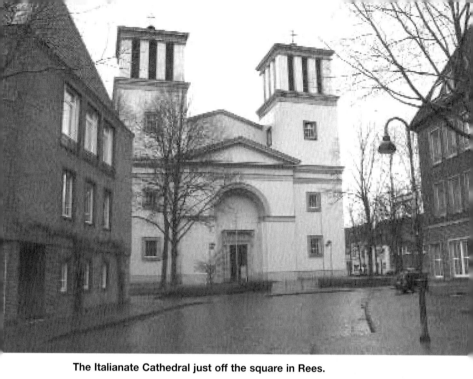

**The Italianate Cathedral just off the square in Rees.**

*It was bitter fighting, street by street and house by house. Early on, a young officer in Aldo Campbell's company, whose first action it was, was hit in the stomach; the command of his platoon devolved on to one Corporal Greaves, an Englishman.*

**A personal snap of *Fallschirmjäger* fighting amongst the rubble in 1945.**

*Campbell asked him if he was quite confident about commanding the platoon; Greaves replied that he didn't know much about it, but 'you just show me where to go and I'll go.' And so he did, to some tune throughout the night; wherever Aldo Campbell told him to go, he went, and took his platoon with him.*

The fighting went on all night and into the next morning. Houses were changing hands; the Germans were using *Panzerfausts* at close range in the rubble-filled streets so effectively, that the tanks and the fuel filled Wasp flame-throwers were vulnerable and had to be withdrawn.

Despite General Horrocks' demands, it was obvious that 5 BW's wide sweeping approach would take a considerable time to get anywhere near the station, and that the attack on the enemy strong point was more likely to take place at first light the following morning. Consequently, Colonel Grant-Peterkin decided, on his own initiative, to delay the start of the Gordon's attack until 2100 hours and then to midnight on word of slow progress by 5 BW. In his post operational report, he stressed 'how quickly troops get tired operating amongst rubble caused by the bombardment'.

Without the town being cleared, as feared by the Corps Commander, German assault guns concentrated their fire against the bridging operations on the banks of the Rhine, whilst well-placed observers directed mortar fire onto any troop movements on the open approach to the town. To the British, it was obvious that the Germans were using the Cathedral and Mullenturm (Mill Tower) as observation posts.

Despite their failure to comply with General Horrocks' instructions, the Gordons had used the time well in order to consolidate their company positions and reduce isolated pockets of enemy in the part of the town they had already captured. By dusk, at 1900 hours, the Gordons' situation was, consequently, more secure and the enemy's ability to interfere with the forthcoming night operations, was considerably reduced. In short, Colonel Grant-Peterkin, the man on the ground, had defied his own commander's instructions and it is recorded that the inactivity was concealed, when at:

*2100 hours, night operations had officially started. The battalion however was in fact still resting, so Brigade HQ was kept happy by a series of periodical progress reports indicating that things were going slowly – according to plan.*

**The Mullenturm on the eastern outskirts of Rees dominated the river and much of the town.**

Major Lindsay, the second-in-command, manning the rear link to Brigade recalled: 'It was a little tricky trying to give periodical progress reports about operations that were not taking place!'

At 2200 hours, sustained shelling of the Gordons in Rees and the riverbank beyond by heavy calibre German guns was reported. At the same time, the Black Watch reported that their operations towards the station had started and that 'progress was satisfactory against some opposition'.

During the long night, Major Lindsay was one of those:

> ... who were able to turn in for a few hours during the night and slept rather unevenly as the artillery, just across the river, were going great guns all night. In fact I dreamed that a huge demon of a gunner was lashing the crews with a gigantic whip, crying faster, you so-and-sos, faster.

## The Second Day

By midnight, twelve infantry battalions of XXX Corps had crossed the Rhine along with approximately thirty DD Shermans. However, with the Germans in Rees still holding out artillery with fire being directed from the Cathedral and

Mullenturm disrupting bridging and supply operations, the town had become a focal point of the Divisional Artillery. To the north 2 Seaforth were still fighting in the factory area and to the east, 5/7 Gordons, having cleared the island formed by the Alter Rhine, were pinned down by heavy mortar fire. Consequently, they were unable to contribute to the clearance of the town from the rear.

At 0020 hours, 5 BW reported that the northern part of the town was now clear of enemy, except for the area of the station, which they reported was a well developed strongpoint. An hour and twenty minutes later, 5 BW reported 'slow progress against a determined enemy established in the top floors of houses in the vicinity of the station and the post office'.

With the report that the northern part of the town was substantially clear, Colonel Grant-Peterkin committed A Company to a preliminary operation, starting at 0100 hours. The Company moved off to occupy rubble to the west of the main north-south road in preparation for operations next morning. Within thirty minutes, under the cover of darkness they had partly completed their task, holding positions at the southeast corner of the square. C Company carried out a similar function north of the market place, 'pushing forward through the rubble meeting surprisingly little opposition'.

By first light (0531 hours), however, the Gordons had to report to Brigade HQ that they were making only limited progress.

**The long but relatively narrow Market Square in the centre of Rees, then a German killing area.**

*B Company is unable to cross the lateral because of the fire fight around the station. C Company reports a lot of snipers in the area of the Market Place [square] and Cathedral Square which makes any advance in that direction appear suicidal.*

In full daylight, C Company turned south, and set about going around the Market Place and then clearing down to the riverbank.

It was at this point that the Gordons were to able bring into action a troop of 454 Mountain Battery from 3rd Mountain Regiment Royal Artillery, commanded by Captain James McNair. The 3.7-inch mountain guns, attached to the Battalion for this operation were the only artillery that could cross the river in an amphibious Weasel. Until the bridges had been built, these were the only heavy weapons available in the direct fire role for street fighting. The Sherman DDs could not negotiate the rubble in the town and had already been seen to be extremely vulnerable (even if they had not been needed to repel counter-attacks around Speldrop and Bienen) but the 3.7-inch guns could be taken apart and manhandled into position.

C Company reported that sniper fire was coming from a building near the south east corner of the Market Place about 100 yards from their position. Captain McNair, who had not been in action before, was ably assisted by his troop sergeant, Sergeant White, and 'set about impressing Scots and Germans alike as they brought a gun rapidly into action in clear view of the enemy'. In the excitement and tension of the moment, the gun was fired without the range having been set and the shell detonated short of the target. 'The snipers no doubt believed the next shot would be closer as all enemy firing in that vicinity ceased immediately, signalling another enemy withdrawal.'

A Company were eventually able to cross the main lateral road at about 0700 hours, unhindered, as 5 BW were closing in on enemy positions around the station. Charging across the road, A Company was able to capture the block of buildings

**A 3.7-inch mountain gun and Jeep tractor combination.**

immediately to the west of the main and was now in a position to support an attack on an enemy strongpoint and artillery observation post in the Cathedral.

Immediately A Company had reorganised themselves and deployed into fire positions, D Company, personally led forward by Major Petrie, assaulted the Cathedral. 'Despite strong opposition, the momentum of the attack rapidly quelled all resistance and the position was in turn captured.' Major Lindsay wrote:

**Major Lindsay who took command in mid battle.**

> It all sounds very easy when one writes it down, but this was far from being so. The clearing of every single house was a separate little military operation requiring a special reconnaissance, plan and execution. And the enemy were resisting fiercely all the time with Spandaus, bazookas and snipers, and only withdrawing a little further back at the last moment when their position became untenable.

Meanwhile, at 0900 hours 5 BW had finally reduced the enemy strongpoint in the station to the north of the town. It had been a protracted fight and proved to be similar to the enemy's last stand in the eastern sector of the town later in the day. The Jocks facing a fanatical enemy, who were surrounded, would typically secure a foothold in a building but would be promptly counter-attacked. Having seen off the enemy and secured a firm hold on a building, the remaining, often isolated, *Fallschirmjäger* would continue to resist, while others would infiltrate back into the buildings over the roofs, through attics, cellars and mouse holes. Controlling the men and the battle, clearing and then holding gains consumed manpower and was desperately slow. Eventually, the Black Watch succeeded in taking a handful of prisoners, mostly wounded.

During what was thought to be the final clearance of the town, a shell splinter wounded Colonel Grant-Peterkin as he arrived at his new Tactical HQ, set up in a house in the south west corner of the town. The second-in-command, Major Martin Lindsay, wrote:

> After breakfast, Grant-Peterkin decided to move our command post down to a large cellar in a house in the nearest

*street in Rees, half a mile from us. He went on with the wireless
set and one or two officers, leaving me to bring on the remainder
of the men and vehicles in my own time. Soon after they had left,
two or three salvoes of fairly heavy shells came down between us
and the new HQ and I hoped they had been able to reach it in
time. I put off our departure for about twenty minutes, by which
time peace reigned again.*

When Major Lindsay and his group reached the cellar at the
edge of Rees, he was greeted by the bad news:

*'The Colonel has been hit,' and there he was, sitting in a chair,
saying he was quite all right but looking pretty green. I sent for
our doctor, who said he had a small fragment in the ribs, and that
of course he ought really to go back, but he didn't think it had
penetrated, in which case he would be all right. I said: 'For God's
sake go back, for you will only cramp my style if you are going
to sit at my elbow while I command the battalion', which perhaps
was not very well put. He replied, 'No, you go down and see how
the companies are, and I will stay by the wireless set.' Half an
hour later, the Adjutant rang me up to say that the Colonel
wasn't feeling well at all and had allowed himself to be
evacuated.*

The situation in mid-morning, thirty-six hours after the crossing
of the Rhine, Major Lindsay summed up on taking command:

*... the companies had all taken their limited objectives of the
night before, and D and C Companies had reached the Cathedral
and cleaned up all the waterline as far as that, but the enemy
were still resisting fiercely in what was still rather more than
one-third of the town.*

The official battalion report detailed the location and situation
of the individual companies, as follows:

*a.  A Company were moving across the middle of the town to
clear the area between Station Road and the cathedral.*

*b.  B Company were moving along the river bank and meeting
opposition from within the town but the waterfront was being
cleared of enemy.*

*c.  C Company was acting as anchor and occupied the
cathedral square. The Company HQ was in the SW corner where
Major Lindsay moved up to conduct the remainder of the
operations.*

*d.  D Company were just south west of the cathedral covering
the rear of B Company. One of the platoon commanders,*

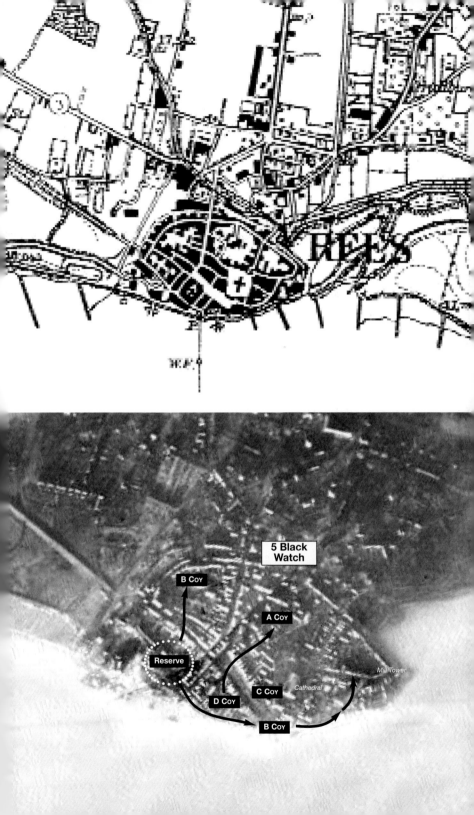

*Lieutenant Porter had been killed, by the same salvo that hit the CO, having already been injured by a* Schumine *during the previous evening.*

C Company HQ was in the corner house opposite the Cathedral Square, which is where Major Lindsay decided to command the remainder of the battle. In a difficult environment to exercise command and control, the Gordons' tactical HQ was sited well forward in the centre of the town at an easy to find location.

The final organised enemy resistance on the riverbank was in the old Mill Tower, which was captured by B Company. With the last position overlooking the Rhine removed, the Royal Engineers were now able to carry out their much-delayed bridging operations immediately south of Rees, unhindered by enemy fire.

The battle was, however, not over for B Company, who turned north to clear up the remainder of the town. They ran into very stiff opposition from a machine gun in a concrete pillbox at a crossroads a hundred yards north of the Cathedral. This enemy position was supported by *Fallschirmjäger* hidden in the houses along the approach road from the south. During this phase of the battle, three B Company officers became casualties.

*Lieutenant Halleron was shot in the back by a sniper and died; Second Lieutenant Macdonald was mortally wounded by a burst of* Spandau *fire from the pillbox and Lieutenant Burnel, a B Company spare officer called up to replace Halleron less than an hour earlier, was shot in the head and appeared to be severely wounded. Major Morrison was himself hit on the head by sniper fire but his helmet deflected the round and he was uninjured.*

Captain McNai, was again in action; having helped to rescue one of the officers, he set about dealing with the enemy positions. Captain Bill McFarlan took him up to a position which overlooked the enemy-held

**Hitlerjugend soldier prepares to throw a stick grenade.**

buildings. Meanwhile, the mountain gunners manhandled bits of the 3.7-inch gun up the stairs and set it up. McNair was demanding to know which window the sniper was using, so McFarlan took a large mirror off the wall and held it out of the window and the *Spandau* gunner obligingly fired at the reflection. 'With no more than "Oh, that one" for a comment he gave orders for the gun to be dragged forward and, laid his gun and fired' setting the house on fire and destroying the enemy *Spandau* position. With this success, B Company looked for a repeat performance from the gunners. By again carrying pieces of the gun and its ammunition (each round weighed twenty-one pounds) through the rubble, McNair and his mountain gunners eventually found a spot from which he could engage the pillbox and knocked it out with several well-placed shots.

Major Lindsay recalled that McNair's:

> ... *enthusiasm for battle ... can seldom have been seen before – in fact it was rather easy for some of our more battle weary officers to be quite funny about it. For each situation in this street to street battle, McNair had some excellent suggestion for using his gun. He hauled it over rubble, rushed it around corners, laid it on a house that was giving trouble, dodged back again, prepared his charges and then ran back to fire them...*

> *This very brave officer took incredible risks; finally, he ran out into a street, which was under fire and pulled in a wounded officer.*

Captain McNair RA and his gun were soon the talk of the division and 'in a few hours, had become an almost legendary character'and received a well-deserved Military Cross.

After this action, the *Fallschirmjäger* withdrew to their final pre-prepared defensive position, which was only a hundred yards square, sited around an ancient fortification on the extreme eastern edge of the town. Here they had well-prepared trenches and a large concrete casemate. B Company closed in but they were driven into cover by the fire of a determined enemy.

At midday General Horrocks visited the Battalion and congratulated them on a job well done, however, he stressed how vital it was for the position to be fully cleared as soon as possible. Tanks were to be brought up in support of B Company, 1 Gordons in their attack on the final strongpoint in the early afternoon. However, the attack had to be delayed, as the rubble-

The area of the German's final stand on the eastern outskirts of Rees.

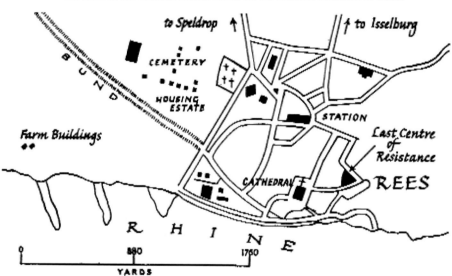

choked streets prevented the tanks from getting into position to support the infantry. Since an attack from the south without armoured support would prove very costly, it was eventually decided that C Company should move so that they could attack from the north through the 5 BW's positions in darkness. At dusk, C Company was poised to make the final attack. The *Fallschirmjäger* commander, *Hauptmann* Hubner, had, however, already told all his fit men to disperse and break through the cordon set up by 1 Gordons and 5 BW.

With B Company about to attack, *Hauptmann* Hubner approached the company under a white flag and asked to surrender and made it plain that he wished to see Major Lindsay in order to negotiate terms for the treatment of his wounded men. The acting CO recalled:

> *He was marched in front of me as I sat at my table poring over the map, and gave me a spectacular Hitler salute, which I ignored ... He was a nasty piece of work, cocksure and good looking in a flashy sort of way, but I had to admire the brave resistance which he had put up. The strain of the battle was apparent in the black chasms under his eyes. He said that they had left eight badly wounded men in two dug-outs.*

Hubner apparently complained that a Jock had relieved him of his wallet when he had surrendered but Lindsay was of the opinion that having looted most of Europe, the Nazis could expect little else in return!

**Rees after its capture.**

While these negotiations were taking place and complaints were being dealt with, a B Company platoon, led by Captain Bill Macfarlane entered the strongpoint and found it clear of active enemy. 'It was a great moment when at 10 p.m. we were able to send the signal that the town was clear.'

So ended a battle that had lasted for almost forty-eight hours resulting in the capture of two officers and 124 other ranks from the *Fallschirmjäger* and *Volkssturm*. A similar number were killed or wounded and some escaped to the north east in the dark. On the other hand, 1 Gordons' losses totalled sixty-two officers and men.

The defenders of Rees, who probably never exceeded 500 Germans of mixed quality, had prevented 5/7 Gordons crossing the Alter Rhine until midnight on D+1 and had drawn a second battalion (5 Black Watch) into the fight. *Hauptmann* Hubner had in effect, fixed all three battalions of 153 Brigade at a time when troops east of the Rhine were at a premium and badly delayed XXX Corps operations and, it could be argued, held up its advance for nearly two days. *Hauptmann* Hubner and his elite and far from elite force had done their job well. Sadly for them their comrades fared less well in their endeavours to destroy the Allied bridgeheads.

**The fighting over, a British despatch rider makes his way through the ruined streets of Rees.**

# CHAPTER 9

# The Capture of Speldrop and Bienen

IN CHAPTER 4, WE LEFT 1 Black Watch of 154 Brigade, mid-morning on 23 March, having been forced back from Speldrop by a vigorous German counter-attack and had only just managed to retain a foothold in Klein Esserden. As far as XXX Corps was concerned Speldrop and Bienen were key to breaking out of the bridgehead that was hemmed in by the Alter Rhine. Colonel Stacey the Canadian official historian explained the significance of the village:

*To expand northward therefore the villages of Speldrop and*

**See air photo on page 226**

*Bienen must be taken. Speldrop itself lies at the heel of the great horseshoe of which the Alter Rhein is the western side. Bienen at the northern end is the toe of the horseshoe and the waters of the Millinger Meer form the eastern side. A breakout could only be accomplished by securing Bienen, but Bienen could not be taken so long as the Germans held Speldrop.*

The Germans had fully appreciated the tactical value of these villages and were determined to hold them knowing that the British needed to take them to expand the bridgehead. A second attempt was made by 1 Black Watch, now supported by tanks of the Staffordshire Yeomanry and two of the Battalion's Wasp flame-throwers. They were quickly in possession of Klein Esserden and then turned against Speldrop, 'but could not get across the open ground without loss, and their attack failed'.

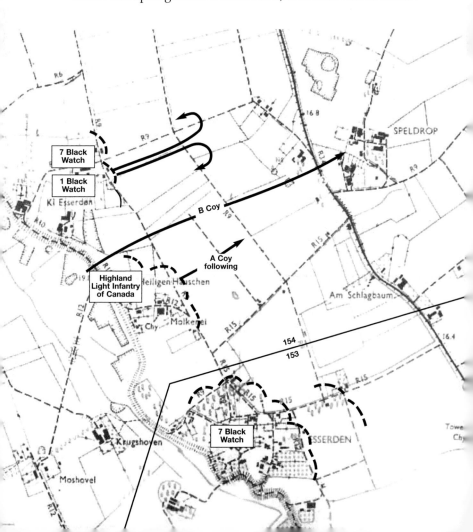

**The Royal Artillery Rocket Battery preparing to fire across the Rhine during Operation PLUNDER.**

### Speldrop

The Black Watch's third attack on 24 March against Speldrop went in at 1630 hours, with the infantry advancing behind a creeping barrage of smoke and HE. The regimental historian records that 'At first it fared well and even got a footing; but eventually it was expelled, leaving another platoon isolated and stranded'. Under cover of a smoke screen, the battered Jocks of the Black Watch withdrew, leaving their wounded sheltering in the cellars. One of the stranded platoons in Speldrop was successfully contacted by radio and told to take what cover they could from their own division's artillery fire.

In the late afternoon, the leading Canadian battalion, the Highland Light Infantry of Canada, commanded by Lieutenant Colonel Strickland, was ordered to take Speldrop, instead of Bienen, which had been nominated as their original task. Their war diary recorded:

> The attack by HLI of C was to be well supported; six field and two medium regiments, as well as two heavy batteries (7.2s) were available to back up our attempt to gain the village of Speldrop. At 1600 hours, behind a series of linear artillery concentrations and with the left flank screened by smoke to give

221

**A *Fallschirmjäger* gun position officer receives fire orders to stop the Canadian advance.**

*protection against the German fire from the north, B Coy HLI of C went in from the west.*

With the artillery keeping the enemy's heads down, a single company of Canadians advanced across 1200 yards of flat, 'horribly open fields', which despite the smoke screen were swept by the enemy's machine guns, artillery and mortar fire. A member of the battalion recalled, 'Hugging the shelter of our own barrage, the leading company reached the outskirts of the built-up portion of the town but immediately ran into stiff resistance'. The CO believed that by sending B Company on its own he would be reducing casualties from both friendly and enemy fire. If an eighty-strong company could break into the village and establish a firm base, the remainder of the battalion could follow in stages with covering fire. This approach worked well at Speldrop but Sergeant Reidel led a bayonet charge against enemy positioned in an orchard and then led his men on through the outskirts of the village. The rest of the company followed Sergeant Reidel, who surprised Major King by promptly handing over the three troublesome 75 mm anti-tank guns and their crews as prisoners.

Having reached the edge of the village Major King realised that he needed the HLI of C's six-pounder anti-tank guns, as the enemy had moved a platoon of assault guns into Speldrop in support of the *Fallschirmjäger*. In addition, he requested the Wasp flame-throwers, which had been brought across the river aboard LVTs, to help him burn the enemy out of buildings. The Wasps however, had a strictly limited supply of flame fuel and would only be able to deal with a few buildings before withdrawing to refuel. B Company used this close support to help storm the German position and secure a lodgement amongst the buildings on the northern edge of the village.

With B Company having broken into Speldrop, A Company was then brought across the open ground to join the fight against the determined *Fallschirmjäger*, who were defending the fortified houses. The Wasp flame-throwers negated the *Fallschirmjäger*'s defensive advantage to a degree. A member of the Battalion recalled that 'even the resolution of these well trained toughs melted before the horrid jets of flame which the Wasps sprayed among them, and the backbone of their resistance was broken'. Meanwhile, C Company succeeded in clearing the southern part of the town extricating the trapped platoons of 1 Black Watch, while the fourth rifle company sent patrols north of the town and captured several *Fallschirmjäger* machine-gun crews who were,

**The Wasp flame-thrower, a converted carrier, is filled with flame fuel.**

curiously enough, asleep at their guns. Colonel Stacey noted that 'It was evident that the past twenty-four hours of almost continual attack and bombardment had rendered the German infantry completely exhausted'.

The HLI of C's war diary reads:

> The battle continued well into the morning of the 25th. Houses had to be cleared at the point of the bayonet and single Germans made suicidal attempts to break up our attacks ... It was necessary to push right through the town and drive the enemy out into the fields where they could be dealt with.

One of the factors in downgrading German performance in Speldrop was the presence of the isolated Black Watch Platoons. Sergeant Johnson commanded one of the platoons and received a DCM for his part in the battle. The *Fallschirmjäger* had repeatedly fought their way into the platoon's house before being ejected. When relieved, the Jocks counted thirty-five dead Germans around the house.

### Bienen 24 – 25 March 1945

While the HLI of C was mopping up the last resistance in and around Speldrop, 7 Argylls were ordered to pass through 1 BW in Klein Esserden and to capture Bienen. The Battalion attacked Bienen in the fading light, but as at Speldrop numerous, well-prepared and still determined Germans, supported by *panzers* and assault guns opposed the Scots. It was obvious that *15th Panzergrenadiers* had taken over responsibility for holding the vital ground of Bienen.

The soldiers of B Company, who were acutely aware that they were facing self-propelled guns, delivered the Argyll's first

**Argyll Farm.**

Bienen

7 A&SH

*Fallschirmjäger* **MG 42 team firing from cover.**

**Lieutenant Colonel Mac-Kinnon, CO 7th Argylls.**

attack from the southwest and reported that 'enemy *spandau* posts were chattering away all along the Bund'. Their historian describes the attack:

*A platoon under Lieutenant Maxwell tried to rush a farm and were never seen again. It was discovered later that the farm was held by at least fifty Boche. B company commander, Major Morton, along with all the platoon officers was wounded, and the company sergeant major was killed. After a grim battle, B Company had eventually to be withdrawn to A Company's position at Rosau.*

At 2000 hours, in full darkness, the Argylls tried again, this time with D Company advancing across the open ground to Bienen, illuminated by German mortar flares that spiralled down from above. D Company had 'a very sticky time', and most of the *Spandau* posts had to be taken at the point of the bayonet. By

225

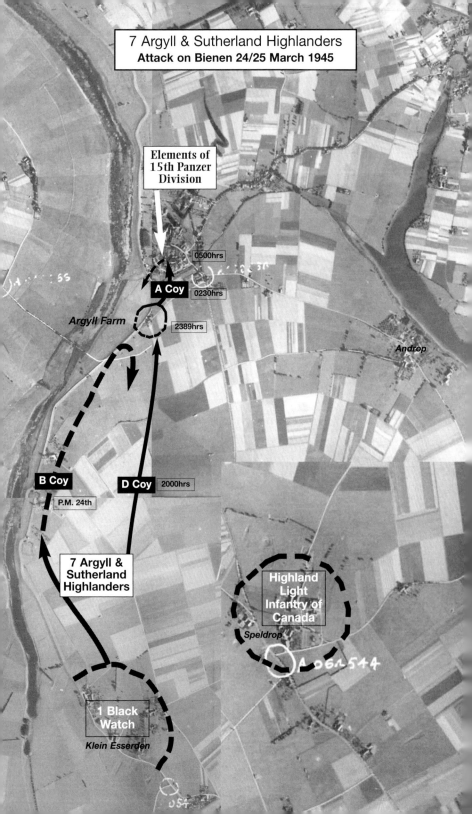

7 Argyll & Sutherland Highlanders
**Attack on Bienen 24/25 March 1945**

Elements of
15th Panzer
Division

0500hrs

**A Coy**  0230hrs

*Argyll Farm*  2389hrs

*Androp*

**B Coy**  **D Coy**  2000hrs

P.M. 24th

7 Argyll &
Sutherland
Highlanders

Highland
Light
Infantry
of
Canada

*Speldrop*

**1 Black
Watch**

*Klein Esserden*

about midnight 24/25 March, the farm at the southwest corner of Bienen had been taken, along with sixty prisoners, mostly from the *15th Panzergrenadier Division*. Lieutenant Colonel MacKinnon's plan was now to pass A Company through D Company. They were to attack to the southern half of Bienen and if successful, B Company was then to go through D Company and clear the northern half of Bienen.

Meanwhile, Bienen was subjected to heavy artillery fire and at 0230 hours, A Company advanced from Rosau, supported by a troop of DD tanks from the Staffordshire Yeomanry, who engaged suspected targets on the edge of the village in an effort to suppress the enemy fire.

*After passing through D Company, A Company immediately ran into very heavy opposition from* Spandaus *and self-propelled guns mostly sited along the southern edge of Bienen. The tank troop commander was killed, and Lieutenant Laurie, one of our platoon commanders, was wounded. Everything possible was tried to get into Bienen, but without success. Finally, A Company tried an outflanking movement to the right with one platoon. They had, however, only gone a short distance when they again ran into withering machine-gun fire.*

In the early hours of 25 March, Brigadier Oliver had concluded that it was not possible to capture Bienen with just 'one or two companies' and the attack was broken off leaving the Argylls with a toe hold in Bienen at the west corner of the village. After some discussion and hot planning by the divisional staff, it was decided that one of the Canadian battalions would renew

**Brigadier Oliver.**

227

the attack in daylight. Before the Canadians could arrive, the *Panzergrenadiers* launched a quick counter-attack to drive the Argylls out of their positions on the edge of the village around 0500 hours. Major Ian Cameron wrote, 'Heavy defensive fire was brought down continuously and the counter-attack was broken up'.

By dawn, 7 A & SHs' two attacks and the German counter-attack had resulted in heavy losses and they had been beaten back to the farm buildings several hundred yards from the southwest corner of the village. In addition to casualties during operations earlier in the day, the exhausted Argylls had lost seven officers and ninety-six other ranks.

The force needed to capture Bienen was already on its way, in the form of 9 Canadian Infantry Brigade, whose other battalions were now on the east bank of the Rhine. The Stormont Dundas & Glengary Highlanders (SD&GH) had crossed first in Buffaloes the previous afternoon and had concentrated near the river south-east of Speldrop and the North Nova Scotia Highlanders (North Novas) followed at 1700 hours using the storm boat ferry service, and concentrated in the area recently vacated by HLI of C.

With these extra battalions available, General Horrocks redeployed his forces. This saw the SD&GH relieve 7 BW in the area of Reeserward, between the main river and the Alter Rhine. This move together with those described below meant that Brigadier Rockingham's 9 Canadian Brigade had taken over the Highland Division's left flank. The Reeserward position was very exposed but the Canadians:

> ... *taking advantage of whatever cover the moonlit night offered, moved in. Once in place, they found themselves occupying the unique position of the extreme left of the whole Allied force which had crossed the Rhine.*

The relief completed, 7 BW moved to a concentration area northwest of Ratshof, leaving the SD&GH to plan an attack on Grietherbusch which was to be delivered at dawn on 25 March.

With the failure of 7 A&SH to capture Bienen and because of the mauling they had received, a fresh battalion, the North Novas, were ordered forward through Speldrop to renew the attack at 0900 hours. Following behind the North Novas, 1 BW

**Infantry deployed in an open assault formation await the signal to advance across some open ground.**

was to relieve the centre HLI of C in Speldrop. This Canadian battalion reorganised and became the Brigade reserve with immediate effect. The final move was bringing the North Shore Regiment over to join 9 Canadian Brigade in order to give depth to the bridgehead and be available to exploit opportunities.

The day started well for the Canadians with the SD&GH attacking Grietherbusch with great dash. By 1200 hours 25 March, the enemy, 'despite suicidal stands along the road from Grafenhof to the farm at Tillhaus, had been subdued', and the SD&GH were probing forward in search of further resistance. In the centre of the divisional area, however, the Canadians were to face a far sterner test.

### Bienen – Operation ASTER

In his notes on operations on 25 March, the Canadian official historian noted:

*This was the Novas first battle on the east bank of the Rhine, and as if to show the significance of this action, the war diary of this veteran unit contains the heading 'The day of the battle 25 Mar 45'; as though everything else which had befallen since 6 June 44 was as*

229

**A 25-pounder of 43 Wessex Division firing in support of 9 Canadian Brigade.**

*nothing compared to this costly day.*

At 0530 hours on 25 March, in an observation post overlooking the open ground between Speldrop and the vital village of Bienen Colonel Forbes gave his orders to the Company Commanders. He started by outlining their part in XXX Corps' Plan. The task of North Novas was to pass through 7 A&SH, capture the village and thus open the way for a northward expansion of the bridgehead, which would free the ferries and forward assembly areas from shell and mortar fire and open the roads for the breakout into the heart of Germany.

The plan for the battalion attack was divided into two phases, with H Hour at 0900 hours. The first problem was to get the attacking troops across three hundred yards of open country and to help with this support by heavy artillery fire, including plenty of smoke fired by both field guns and the battalion's 3-inch mortars. According to the Battalion's War Diary:

> *In the first phase A Company would seize the right hand portion of the village and B the left, thus securing the start line for C and D Companies in the next phase, in which the east and*

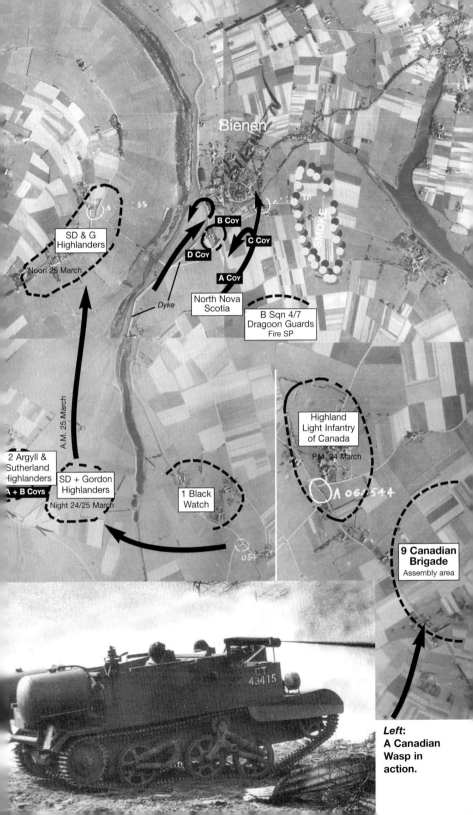

Bienen

SD & G
Highlanders

Noon 25 March

B Coy

C Coy

D Coy

A Coy

North Nova
Scotia

Dyke

SMOKE

B Sqn 4/7
Dragoon Guards
Fire SP

A.M. 25 March

Highland
Light Infantry
of Canada

P.M. 24 March

2 Argyll &
Sutherland
Highlanders
A + B Coys

SD + Gordon
Highlanders

Night 24/25 March

1 Black
Watch

A 064544

9 Canadian
Brigade

Assembly area

CT
434415

*Left*:
A Canadian
Wasp in
action.

**Tension is etched in the faces of these infantrymen in an urban setting.**

*west portions of the rest of the village would be taken. In the first phase a troop of tanks, (B Squadron 4/7 Dragoon Guards), which had been ferried across the Rhine the previous evening, were to support A Company.*

A report on the battle in a Nova Scotia newspaper described the ground that their local men had to cross before they could start the fight to clear Bienen.

*A succession of farms provided very limited amount of cover up the line of the dyke approaching the village from the south. There was no cover whatsoever further to the right or to the left of the Dyke. The next farm [Argyll Farm] was about four hundred yards ahead of the village and the ground beyond was raked by machine-gun fire. The whole area, including the last two farms was under fairly continuous artillery fire and sporadic bursts of machine-gun fire from the right flank. All approaches for vehicles were covered by anti-tank guns.*

The operation did not start well. Major Learment led A

Supporting infantry take cover as the Sherman they were following 'brews up' after taking a direct hit.

The RMO's Jeep and later ambulance Jeeps were the only vehicles across the Rhine until ferries were established.

**Field Marshal Montgomery, Generals Horrocks and Thomas discuss the battle.**

Company up to its start line in single file along the side of the dyke to 'Argyll Farm' but at 0825 hours, thirty-five minutes before H Hour, A Company and the accompanying tanks reported that they were pinned down on their way to the start line by machine guns, snipers and some mortaring. Shortly afterwards, B Company reported that it was experiencing great difficulties in reaching their start line near the farm, still held by the Argylls. Both companies were suffering casualties but 'At 0845 hours, however, the smoke from the supporting fire plan began, and using it for temporary protection, the troops managed to make headway and succeeded in forming up for the attack'.

Having formed up under these adverse conditions and set off, the two companies immediately came under fire from previously unidentified positions and within minutes Colonel Forbes was hearing over the radio that his men were again pinned down, that some of the platoons were out of contact and that casualties were mounting. A and B Companies fell back to

234

the cover of Argyll farm. The Novas' war diary reads:

> ... *the Battalion had quite definitely lost the initiative and contact between platoons was next to impossible because of the murderous fire and heavy mortaring'.*

The next diary entry recorded that:

> *The Commanding Officer contacted Major Learment, A Company Commander, at 0920 hours and asked him to tee up a new attack immediately with the tanks and artillery supported in by his Forward Observation Officer, and make a concerted effort to reach the first row of houses. However, by 1000 hours, nothing had been tied in because so many of the platoons were out of contact and it was impossible to get any sort of message to them.*

The companies eventually attacked again but 'even though attempts were made to reorganise and press on loss of contact and casualties among officers and NCOs made control a serious problem'. At 1145 hours on 25 March, Brigadier Rockingham came forward to make an appreciation and was forced to concede that he would have to use fresh troops to break into Bienen. He directed Colonel Forbes that he was to 'start from scratch and do the attack over again using the two remaining companies'. Armour and artillery fire support was clearly needed in quantity so as to overcome the *Fallschirmjäger* and *Panzergrenadiers* in the vital Bienen position. The battalion's war diary recorded:

An infantryman fires a burst from his Sten before entering a house in the final phase of the clearance.

> *The artillery fire plan was again set up, which consisted of a series of concentrations and stonks on the rear of the town and targets covering the approaches from the rear. Each company had a section of sappers and a forward observation officer while MMGs were laid on targets. The 3-inch mortars were to use smoke and HE to shield the right flank of C Company from observation and fire from Androp. The Typhoons were put in on*

17-pounder self-propelled Archers were ferried across the Rhine and were available to give support to the attacking infantry. They were to take on the German assault guns with a rare qualitative advantage.

**While the Canadians were in action soldiers of 5 Dorset led 43 Wessex Division across the Rhine into the bridgehead.**

*Millingen. The Artillery plan started at H-10 ...*

Colonel Forbes also called for additional armoured support and received an additional troop of four Shermans from B Squadron 4/7 Dragoon Guards, who were grouped with C Company, 'while D had the troop of DD tanks, C Company took in a section of Wasps'. The plan was that C and D Companies were to advance as far as they could into the town and then the remnants of A and B Companies would pass through and clear to the far edge of the objective.

The Forming Up Point and Start Line were again at the farm buildings and at 1430 hours, with the artillery fire plan being repeated, C and D Companies advanced to capture what was still the Phase One objective. Under cover of the exploding shells, D Company, on the left, made good progress towards the village using the dyke and the road as their axes of advance. However, just as they reached the edge of the village their company commander, Major Dickson, was wounded and his men had only managed to take the first houses before they were brought to a halt badly disorganised. Nonetheless, they had succeeded in taking almost a hundred prisoners.

Even though they had a more exposed route to Bienen, C Company too reached the village but:

> ... had a large number of men killed getting across. In spite of this, they persisted and gained a foothold, which they were able to expand sufficiently to prevent direct fire from coming on the open ground they had crossed.

Within 15 minutes of H Hour, C Company were reporting that they had reached the first houses and the fringe of the town but had suffered thirty-three casualties in their advance across the five hundred yards of open ground.

The additional tanks and artillery support had done their job in neutralising and forcing the *panzers* and assault guns, which had been reported in Bienen, out of the village. With the Canadians pressing home their attack, they would have certainly fallen prey to the Canadian infantry amidst the buildings and rubble, had they remained. With the enemy armoured threat neutralised, 'The tanks were on the fringe of the town and bringing heavy fire on the centre in support of the infantry'.

Now that neither the enemy infantry nor *panzers* could cover the approaches to the village with small arms fire, at 1530 hours, A and B Companies were able to close up to Bienen, leaving the stretcher-bearers to the grisly task of clearing the open fields of the dead and the wounded. OC C Company wrote in his post operational report:

> The work of stretcher-bearers and jeep-drivers during the attack was particularly commendable. In spite of the fact that two stretcher-bearers were killed by MG fire while attending to

*Fallschirmjäger* prisoners head into captivity after their last-ditch fight to hold Bienen.

*wounded in the open field the remainder carried on with their job
under fire and all wounded were evacuated quickly.*

At 1600 hours, 9 Canadian Infantry Brigade came under the
command of Major General Ivor Thomas's 43rd Wessex
Division, who was to be responsible for the left flank allowing
the Highland Division to concentrate on the centre and right.
General Thomas promptly demanded that the Canadian renew
the attack.

With the Novas having now gathered sufficient combat
power in the village, including Wasps, at 1700 hours another
attack started with the limited objective of completing the
clearance of what had been originally been their Phase One
objective. C Company was ordered to push forward and clear
the remainder of their quarter of the village, which they
reported as complete at approximately 1745 hours and were
ordered to continue to press on through the village before
reorganising and digging-in.

A and B Companies then took over the advance and
methodically set about the task of clearing each and every
building in the main part of the village. It took the remainder of
the day, yielding a mixed bag of *Fallschirmjäger* and
*Panzergrenadier* prisoners. An account by OC B Company gives
a flavour of the fighting:

> *We picked up three tanks and started into the town along the
> left road. The tanks, our big brothers, covered our right flank by
> 'brewing up' each house in turn, while we moved up the left. A
> couple of the boys were hit by snipers firing from the big house,
> so we got a tank to 'brew it up.' 10 Platoon got into the place and
> started to clear it. This made Jerry very unhappy, and he started
> firing through the floors. We finally, with the help of 12 Platoon
> and the moral support of the tanks, got forty prisoners and a
> couple of officers out of the place.*

At about 1815 hours, C Company reported that enemy armour
in the unwelcome form of assault guns, supported by infantry,
were advancing from the north and knocked out two of the
Shermans. The Company was forced to withdraw. Fortunately,
a counter-attack had been anticipated and a troop of 3rd
Canadian Anti-Tank Regiment Archers were already on their
way forward from the heavy ferry sites to help 9 Canadian
Brigade hold their gains. The German attack was prevented
from getting beyond C Company's position when one of the

new Archer SP gun versions of the obsolescent Valentine Tank, mounting a 17-pounder gun, knocked out one of the enemy assault guns.

It had been clear to Brigadier Rockingham for some hours that another battalion was going to be needed and he was under mounting pressure to complete the capture of Bienen. Consequently, the HLI of Canada, were warned that they were to pass through the North Nova Scotias at 2300 hours and 'finish the job'. At 1950 hours, Colonel Forbes ordered the Novas to secure a start line in Bienen for their fellow Canadian highlanders. The Canadian official historian recorded that 'Even this limited task entailed clearing the extensive buildings of a creamery and exploiting to the far end of Bienen', which principally fell to A Company.

For the Novas, the fighting at Bienen on 25 March had been 'a long, hard, bitter fight against excellent troops who were determined to fight to the end'. In this 'day of battle' to kick open the exit from the confined bridgehead, they lost forty-two killed and seventy-nine other ranks wounded.

During the course of the afternoon Brigadier Rockingham was visited by the Corps Commander, General Horrocks, who always liked to visit as far forward as possible. He was briefed that the remainder of 43rd Wessex Division, who 9 Canadian Brigade was still under the command of, was about to cross as a

part of the XXX Corps plan to expand the front by feeding three divisions into the bridgehead. By keeping the frontages narrow sufficient combat power could be applied on the enemy to ensure progress was maintained.

## The Fall of Bienen

The Highland Light Infantry of Canada were to complete the clearance of Bienen supported by the final troop of B Squadron 4/7th Dragoon Guards in order to provide a firm base for the attack of 130 Brigade (43rd Division) to the northeast. Their war diary recorded:

*26 Mar 45. Progress was very slow as the enemy fought like madmen. Isolated houses had to be cleared and proved most difficult. The enemy artillery and mortars poured shells into our troops continually. Again, single paratroopers made suicidal charges at our advancing troops. They were consistently chopped down but often not before they had inflicted casualties on our own sections.*

*By first light, the town had been cleared except for isolated groups of snipers who refused to quit. These were mopped up as D Company pushed through the town to a point at the A/Tk ditch approximately MR 054575. With consolidation completed, the North Shore Regiment under command of 9 Canadian Infantry Brigade passed through us towards Millingen. Lieutenant Colonel J Rowley OC of the North Shore Regiment was killed in this push by enemy Arty fire.*

In their war diary, the HLI of C recorded some of the lessons the battalion had learned in clearing the village: 'When open ground has to be crossed to attack isolated houses we must make use of our supporting arms including an artillery barrage, to block off the flanks as well as hitting the objective.'

Let an entry from a Canadian war diary, referring to Bienen, have the last word on Operation PLUNDER, the Rhine Crossing.

*It was a long hard bitter fight against excellent troops who were determined to fight to the end. It cracked open the bottleneck that had restricted the bridgehead and from then on, the expansion was much easier and more rapid. The road to Northern Germany and Holland was established.*

# CHAPTER 10

# Tours of the PLUNDER Battlefields

THERE ARE THREE SEPARATE Operation PLUNDER tours outlined in this chapter, covering the component operations TURNSCREW, WIDGEON and TORCHLIGHT. Each tour is a distinct entity, and in the case of the first and last named operations will each take at least half a day's touring to complete. The individual tours can, however, be abbreviated and joined as appropriate into a shorter route. The tours are designed for light vehicles up to the size of a small minibus. Ferries, width of roads, size of turning points and weight restrictions all conspire to make a coach tour significantly more difficult and the Germans do not have the same slightly cavalier attitude to road traffic laws as do fellow Europeans further west! Equally, for the car driver I have avoided taking visitors down roads signed *'Anliger Fri'* or access only along with apparently easily motorable roads that are now dedicated to cyclists.

To save space and repetition these tour instructions are brief. Please refer to the text for details of the action.

**General**

In common with many of the battlefields of North-West Europe, time has changed the patterns of human habitation; villages have expanded and roads built or fallen into disuse and on this battlefield, even the ground has changed. In the immediate post war period the rebuilding of the nearby Ruhr and Germany's infrastructure produced an unparalleled demand for aggregate and the Rhine flood plain offered a ready supply of high quality river gravel and sand. Consequently, flooded pits have replaced many of the flood plain's meadows, over which the Second Army advanced on the morning of 24 March 1945. Yet most of the objectives, being on slightly higher ground, are still available for inspection. Away from the flood plain, thanks to the Germans' traditional farming methods, the country has retained much of its original character and did much to extend the scope of this book beyond just the assault phase.

The battles fought by 6th British and 17th US Airborne Divisions will be covered in separate **Battleground** volumes.

## Tour One – Bislich and Haffen (Operation TORCHLIGHT)

This tour covers XII Corps' assault crossing of the Rhine astride the village of Bislich and ends on the Issel. The tour concentrates on the operations of 15th Scottish Division and only covers the airborne action in so much as or where it was directly important to the Scots.

The tour starts in Wesel. Follow the signs to Rees and then to **Fluren** and **Bislich**. Drive through Fluren following the road (**Bislicherstrasse**) through a wooded area, where the Scots met up with the US Paratroopers at 1510 hours on the afternoon of the 24th, and past a large flooded gravel pit. Shortly after a 90 degree bend, in a hamlet (Loh), turn left onto the minor **Westhide** road. Follow this road past a gravel pit and several farms. This is the area cleared by 6 Royal Scots Fusiliers (6 RSF) during 24 March. On reaching a T junction with **Auf der Laak**, turn right, then left and park near the ferry. It is always worth experiencing a crossing of the river and there is a good café on the other side!

This is the area where 44 Lowland Brigade crossed in the LVTs of 11 RTR at 0200 hours on 24 March. 6 RSF crossed a hundred metres down stream and this is the point where the LVT ferry was established to bring subsequent waves across the river. The ferry operates on the site of a pair of class 40 Bailey bridges built by the Royal Engineers. Just up stream was the DUKW ferry point and beyond them were the booms positioned and maintained by the Royal Navy to prevent the enemy from floating mines and barges downstream to wreck the bridges.

Follow the road into **Bislich**, which was secured by 6 King's Own Scottish Borderers, who crossed as the second wave in storm boats. In the centre of the village (look out for an anchor and the **Gaststatte Cramer**), turn left onto **Auf dem Steinberg**. Follow this road out of the village and turn left onto **Drogenkamp**. Park on top of the Dyke. This is the area of the Brigade's storm boat crossing and where a class 9 raft was established, using the track down to the riverbank.

Turn right and follow the dyke road north, past a modern gravel works and stop by three houses on a bend. This is the area of 8 Royal Scots' crossing. Tac HQ was established in the centre house which was subsequently taken over by another unit who stayed for some time. Probably a bank control HQ.

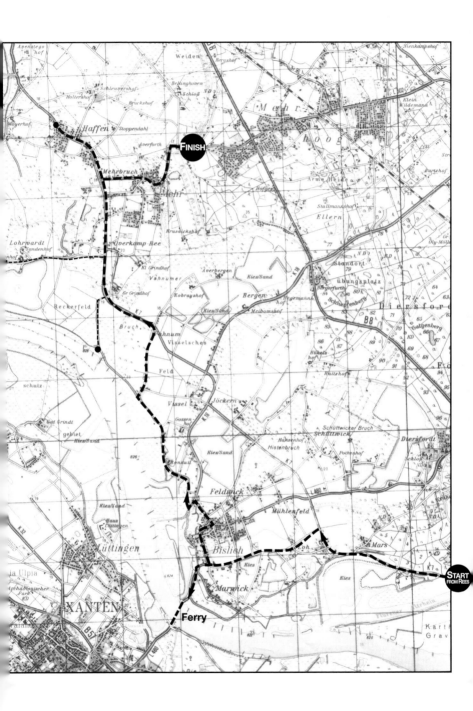

FINISH

START
FROM REES

Ferry

245

Continue on the dyke road for almost half a mile and follow the road inland. On reaching the main road (*Bislicherstrasse*) turn left and left again onto *Am Stummen Deich*, which goes past the wind farm to the river bank where 10 Highland Light Infantry (right assault battalion of 227 Highland Brigade) crossed the river.

Return to the main road and turn left again in 700 metres onto *Lohrwardtestrasse* and follow for two miles to the river bank. This area opposite Vyen was where the remainder of 227 Brigade (2 Gordons and 2 Argylls) came ashore with some difficulty. Hence a considerable gap between 10 HLI and the Argylls.

Return to the main road and turn left to **Haffen**. The village was in the centre of Area Y, 227 Brigade's objective. The open area beyond gives an indication of the difficulties the reinforced 7th *Fallschirmjäger* Division would have had counter-attacking the Scots once they were established in the villages.

Return back down the road towards **Bislich** but turn off left to **Mehr** (1 Km). The village of Mehr was 7 Seaforth's objective and, as elsewhere, the preliminary bombardment and the clearance ensures that there are few original buildings still standing.

## Tour Two – The Wesel Tour (Operation WIDGEON)

This tour concentrates on the Commando action and the capture of the city of Wesel. If coming south from the XII Corps tour or from Wesel, turn off the **B8** into **Fluren** and join the **K7 Bislicherstrasse**. Drive through the village, following the green and white **'Grav Insel'** campsite signs. Turn left off **Bislicherstrasse** and drive down to the campsite entrance.

At weekends and during high season it may be necessary to park and walk the last half mile to the river. Either on foot or by vehicle, follow the concrete block road through the mobile homes and caravans out onto the flood plain. This is the area where 1 Commando Brigade landed. Looking out towards the river, most of the LVTs carrying 46 (first ashore) and 45 RM Commandos and No. 3 Commando landed to the left of the ramp, while No. 6 Commando landed just a little downstream to the right, having crossed in storm boats. Looking east towards Wesel, marked by the Cathedral spire and Needle the flat and open nature of the ground can be easily appreciated. Looking

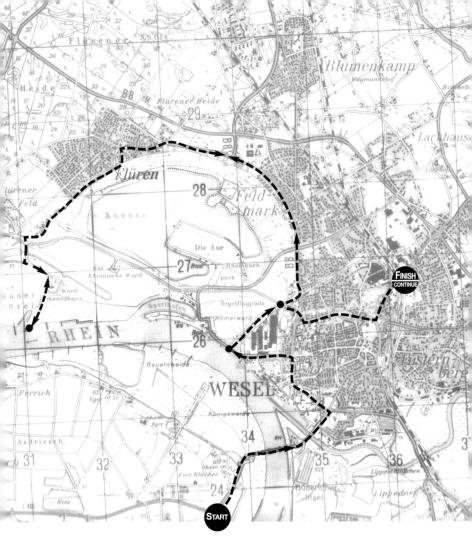

inland, amongst the mobile homes and trees, a brick building can be discerned. This is the **Wardmann's Haus**, objective of B Troop 46 Commando.

Return to **Bisslicherstrasse**. Those wishing walk 6 Commando's two mile route across the flood plain into town, should take the **Deichweg** and the **Rheinwardt** (foot and cycle only). Those following the tour route by car should return through **Fluren** and turn right at the roundabout heading to **Wesel**. The large area of water to be glimpsed through the trees to the right is a large post war gravel pit, the Auesee.

At the **sixth set of traffic lights** (the Germans like traffic lights), turn right onto the **Auedam**. Opposite the **Auestadion** turn right and park. From here, it is a short walk along the top of the dyke to 6 Commando's entry point into Wesel. Alternatively, return to the B8 (**Reeser Landstrasse**), turn right and turn right again at the old railway crossing (just beyond the Aral Garage) onto **Delogstrasse**. Drive parallel to the railway line and park near the point where **Delogstrasse** crosses the railway. The dyke No. 6 Commando followed across the flood plain, is opposite. They entered Wesel through an arch of rails, torn up by the RAF's bombs.

Following **Karl-Jatho-Strasse**, drive past a concrete two storey car park, the **aero club** and the arches beneath the ramp leading up to the old railway bridge. Park near the junction with the riverbank road. Take the steps up the old railway embankment onto a viewing platform on top of a surviving bridge pier. From here, it is easy to appreciate the width of the river and the speed of its current, as well as how Wesel dominated the river up and down stream. To the right is the area where 1 Cheshire crossed the Rhine on the afternoon of 24 March. They went under the remains of the bridge you are standing on and established themselves in the large factory area (with the blue roof) that can be seen through the trees a short distance inland.

Return to the **B8** and the railway crossing. Brigadier Mills-Roberts' plan was to deploy his four commando units along the old railway line facing north. Due to the destruction and post war expansion of Wesel, little remains to be seen of the original battlefield but some of the factories have been repaired/rebuilt.

Turn right onto the B8 and left at the **second set of traffic lights** onto the **Kurfursenring/Herzogenring**. These wide boulevards were less prone to being choked with rubble so were used as axes of advance by the commandos during the detailed clearance of Wesel. Turn left onto **Isseler Strasse** at the fourth set of lights. After two hundred metres park in a side street (**Oststrasse**) and walk up onto the Theodore Heusse Bridge, from where the best view of the factory area can be gained. The last original significant factory building has now been pulled down. Exploring the city centre is not recommended.

To reach the VARSITY area, continue over the bridge and turn left on the **B70 Emericherstrasse**. To continue with Tour

Three turn left out of **Oststrasse** back into town and follow the signs to the **Rhinebrucker** and **Geldern**. Once across the bridge turn right at the first set of traffic lights towards **Kleve**. Whilst crossing this area it is worth stopping to look at the plan showing the organisation of XII Corps' rear area for the assault on page xx. It is also worth considering the problems of camouflaging these preparations and the mass of artillery and its ammunition that was brought forward during the nights preceding the assault. Turn onto the **B57** signed to **Xanten**.

## Tour Three – Rees and the XXX Corps Battlefields (Operation TURNSCREW)

Less popular than an amalgam of the XII Corps/Wesel and the Operation Varsity routes, a tour of the battlefields of Rees, Speldrop and Bienen is none the less well worthwhile. Not only is the ground far less changed; there are few of the sand and gravel pits that spoil the flood plain further south around Wesel. Rees was not as badly damaged and it is also the scene of the most serious opposition to the Second Army's crossing.

This tour starts on the **K45** in the village of **Appeldorn** on the west bank of the Rhine. This was the site of the Forward HQ of 51st Highland Division, which was concealed amongst the substantial houses and farm buildings. It is where Major General Thomas Rennie was initially buried. Follow the **K45** and join the main road heading north east to **Rees (B67)**.

While crossing this modern bridge (there was no bridge here in 1945) the visitor has a good view of 153 Brigade's area of operations; the city of Rees, its cathedral and the low-lying 'island' beyond, where 5/7 Gordon crossed and were pinned down by 7th *Fallschirmjäger* Division. Almost immediately below the bridge and to the left is the scene of 5 Black Watch's crossing.

Continue across the bridge taking a **left turn, at the first traffic lights**, onto a minor road at a crossroads after about a thousand metres. Drive into Esserden and turn left at the T-junction. Follow the road through the village, over a dyke and doubling back on oneself drive down to a T-junction and turn right on the main road signed to **Grithendorf**. Take the next left just before a large river lake (in existence in 1945) and drive down to the river. This is the centre of 154 Brigade's area.

To the left is the site where 7 Argylls crossed at 2200 hours

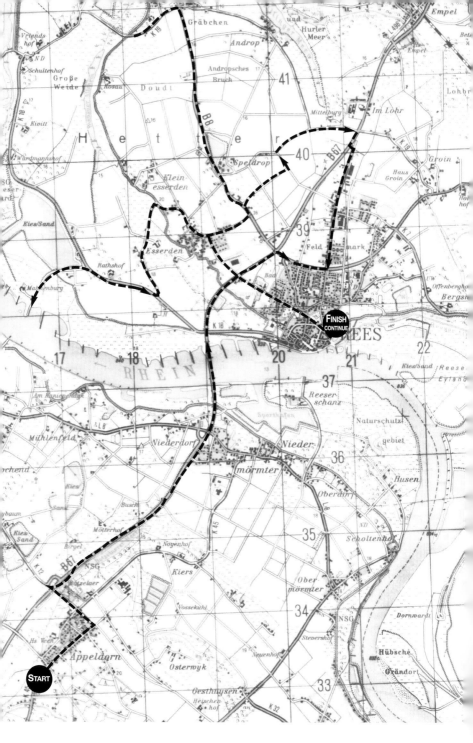

and to the right is the crossing point of 7 Black Watch, who were landed incorrectly astride the channel between lake and river and had to make a lengthy detour before they could assemble. The Black Watch seized the farm of Mahnenburg 150 metres to the right, which they secured from the stunned *Fallschirmjäger* with little difficulty. The slipway on which you are standing is in the area where exits were made for the DD tanks of the Staffordshire Yeomanry, who started to land here after dawn on 24 March. Facing inland is the Ratshof Farm complex, the initial objective of 7 Argylls.

Retrace your route back towards **Esserden** and as you drive up across the dyke look a quarter left. This small collection of farm buildings is **Klein Esserden**, which was the objective of 1 Black Watch, 154 Brigade. Continue on through **Esserden**, which was captured by 5 Black Watch.

Drive east out of old Esserden through the new part of the village and **turn left** on the **B8** heading north to **Speldrop**, which is the loose collection of farms and houses six hundred metres further on. Park in a large lay-by on the left.

Continue along the road towards **Bislich**. Just past the town sign is a left turn. Take the turn and park. There is a small German military cemetery here, with about 150 graves mostly dating from March 1945. Drive on several hundred metres to the point where the road climbs over a dyke. Stop and look back along the dyke towards **Bienen**. The farm on the dyke is Argyll Farm. The dyke was used as the only approach that offered any cover for 7 Argylls and the North Nova Scotia Highlanders.

Return on the **B8** south towards **Rees**, **turn left** 500 metres past Speldrop and stop at the crossroads. This was known as 'Bill'. This open country was crossed by A Company 2 Seaforth and 5 Cameronian to the north, who were to isolate Rees. Turn left and then right and join a larger road driving straight on. A drainage ditch, improved by the Germans as an anti-tank obstacle is crossed. The Seaforth had a stiff fight for this bridge, which was necessary if heavy support weapons and tanks were to be brought forward to support them. **Cross the bridge** and the modern **B67** into the factory area.

Return to the B67 and drive south to **Rees** where we will visit the scene of 2 Gordons' battle for the city. At the **B67/B8** roundabout go straight on (B67) and turn left at the next traffic lights/crossroads, taking a minor road heading towards **Rees**. To the right are the bund and the area crossed by the Gordons on their way to the city under cover of darkness. Park by the junction. The cemetery and housing estate, which were the entry point, are either side of the road.

It's worth parking in this area and continuing the tour of this charming old town on foot (it's small enough) but the route described can be driven. However, there are the usual problems with stopping and parking that bedevil any modern town. If parking, the Lidel car park is recommended!

Continue across the junction following the **Stadtmite** signs. This open area is where the station and a series of large houses converted into a strong point were located. They were both taken by 5 BW on the morning of 26 March.

Still following the **Stadtmite** signs, turn onto **Vor dem Delltor**, which is referred to as the 'North-South Road' in accounts of the battle. Going south down the road, to the right is the area cleared by the Gordons' B and C Companies on the morning of 24 March and the road became in effect no-man's-land until the early hours of the 25th when the Gordons resumed the attack.

Continue down the road until it opens out into the Market Square. The *Fallschirmjäger* had this area covered with fire and Captain MacNair's mountain gun was a considerable help in clearing both houses and ruins around the square. At the bottom of the Market Square and to the left is the Cathedral Square dominated by the bulk of the rebuilt Italianate Cathedral. Just to the right is the scene of the *Fallschirmjägers'* last resistance before they surrendered on the evening of 26 March.

This completes the XXX Corps/Rees tour. If the visitor is heading for the Reichswald, Arnhem or the autobahn system back to the UK take the B67 across the Rees Bridge but if returning to Wesel, take the B8 via Haffen and Bislich.

### THE CEMETERIES

There are several Cemeteries of interest to those studying Operation PLUNDER.

### Reichswald Forest Cemetery

This cemetery is sited within the Reichswald Forest on the road between Kleve in Germany and Gennep in Holland, on the German side of the border. It is the largest CWGC cemetery, in terms of area, and contains 7,654 graves. One hundred and sixty-two of the burials are unknown. There are also 79 graves of other nationalities, most of them Poles who fought with the Polish Armoured Division, as a part of the First Canadian Army.

After the War, thousands of graves of soldiers and airmen were concentrated from burial places across western Germany. Most of the soldiers were killed in the Battle of the Rhineland, some dying fighting in the forest itself in February 1945. A significant number also died during the early stages of Operation PLUNDER, among them are members of the Highland and Scottish Divisions, along with men of 6th British Airborne Division, whose bodies were moved from Hamminkeln. The Army graves are on the right, as one enters the cemetery.

Amongst the dead buried here is Major General Thomas Rennie (plot LXI, row D, grave 1) who lies amongst his beloved Jocks.

Nearly 4,000 airmen are buried in the cemetery. Some lost their lives in supporting the advance into Germany but the majority died during the bomber campaign against targets in Germany, and were brought to the Reichswald from cemeteries in the neighbouring area. Graves were concentrated here from cemeteries in Dusseldorf, Krefeld, Mönchen-Gladbach, Essen, Cologne, Aachen, Dortmund and many other places in the area. Some were first buried in isolated graves where their aircraft crashed; by a roadside, a riverbank, in a garden or a forest.

### Rheinberg War Cemetery
Rheinberg is a small town to the west of the Rhine, three miles from the River and nine miles south of Wesel. The Cemetery is about two miles southwest of the town on the Kamp-Lintfort road. Most of the 3,335 burials were airmen who died in bombing attacks on Germany. Their graves were concentrated here from cemeteries and isolated, wayside graves near where their aircraft crashed. From Cologne alone, over 450 Air Force dead who had been buried by the Germans were re-interred here.

There are also over 400 soldiers buried in the cemetery, many of whom were killed in the Battle of the Rhineland,

Operation PLUNDER and the advance to the Elbe. Among them are West Countrymen and Scots who died in the battle for Goch in February 1945 and others who fell in the stubborn fighting for Lingen, which was cleared by the 3rd Division on 6 April.

## The German Cemeteries

In common with German practice, many of the German dead were subsequently reburied in cemeteries near their next of kin. However, if not visited as a part of the TURNSCREW Tour, there is a small German cemetery at Bislich and a larger one in the Dierfordtenwald on the L480 Bislich to Hamminkeln road just south of the junction with the B8.

**Major General Rennie's grave at Reichswald Forest Cemetery.**

**German cemetery at Bislich with the distinctive heavy cross headstone.**